# Leadership 101

**Developing Leadership Skills** For Resilient Youth

*facilitator's guide*

by Mariam MacGregor

Publisher: Youthleadership.com

Design and Layout:   Michelle Ludt

Leadership 101: Developing Leadership Skills for Resilient Youth
©2000, Mariam MacGregor, Denver, CO

This book has a companion Student Workbook available separately from the publisher.

Ordering Information:
Youthleadership.com
5593 Golf Course Drive
Morrison, CO  80465
Phone: (303) 358-1563
Website: www.youthleadership.com

*about this curriculum*

*Leadership 101* is designed to be taught at the high school level. This curriculum, however, incorporates a significant amount of college-level materials and concepts. It can therefore be modified to use early in a college leadership development program. Likewise, it also can be simplified to use with middle school students. *Leadership 101* is specifically designed to establish a foundation for leadership education programs for adolescents and young adults.

This curriculum presents an adaptable and broad-based perspective of leadership. The population with which it has been implemented and evaluated are diverse, resilient ("at-risk") teenagers. It is clearly appropriate, and has been implemented, with a variety of teen populations. The curriculum also is being used in various community-based organizations and non-school settings with success. Another effective method includes incorporating the activities within mixed adult/youth programs (such as community leadership programs).

This comprehensive facilitator's guide and student workbook take both the instructor and students through various leadership concepts and experiential skill-building activities. In addition to affective components, students have significant academic responsibilities as they explore, practice, and understand their own philosophy of leadership within the school and community setting. In my setting, students also may select to take an advanced leadership course following successful completion of Leadership 101. This higher level course is designed to put "words and skills into action", with the leadership focus shifting each quarter.

Measurement and evaluation is conducted quarterly after students have completed the class. Academic standards are measured by class projects, exams, and participatory leadership both within the class and as demonstrated within the school community. Information is also maintained by tracking retention of students and their participation in school-related and community-based leadership experiences. A pre/post assessment tool is available from the publisher for use with the curriculum

The concept of leadership has been an ongoing challenge. Incorporating this concept into the reality of youth and young adults often demands creativity and innovation. Many of the students with whom I have worked will deny that they are "leaders" even when they clearly have natural leadership qualities. The identity crisis with "leadership" is fascinating if not frustrating, as many young adults have some pretty negative interpretations of leaders and leadership!

The thrill of conducting this class is that the eyes of your students will be opened to how they can be a good leader, as well as what qualities they should look for in leaders. This is an active, experiential class and demands that you be as excited about the concepts and activities as you want the students to be! I have found that students will begin to assess their own behaviors or will reflect on the individuals who they have followed (as leaders or mentors), and will develop more meaningful definitions of leadership and the associated qualities.

Class sessions have been designed for 90 minute meeting times, with a 5 minute break at 45 minutes. If your schedule does not accommodate this, I suggest determining appropriate breaks in activities for each class session. Some of the classes can be easily modified for two 45-50 minute sessions, although for classes which require debriefing immediately, it is wise to structure the class appropriately so that this can be accomplished.

In general, I have effectively distributed points as follows, although any modification is appropriate for your needs:

| | |
|---|---|
| **Reflections** | **15 points each** |
| **Organizational Observation** | **50 points** |
| **Leader Research Paper** | **125 points** |
| **Exams** | **100 points each** |
| **Participation** | **up to 10 points (daily)** |

In the student handbook, there are "Alternate Reflection" pages included for each assignment. This allows you and your students the flexibility to modify reflections. It also allows for alternate assignments in cases where your class gets really turned on by a topic or enters into a hot discussion about the class experiences or related events in your school.

Due to the experiential nature of the class activities, you may find that some students are uncomfortable taking the risks necessary to engage fully in an activity. I strongly encourage you to maintain a "challenge by choice" approach, especially where students indicate that they are not comfortable participating. This usually arises during some of the team building activities. It should be your goal to establish confidence in dealing with peer pressure and personal strengths, not perpetuating peer pressure by making students feel awkward for not participating! For the most part, even students who opt out of some activities still experience a lot and learn from the discussions and application which follow.

## Goals:
- To review outline of class goals and expectations
- To provide introduction to leadership concepts
- To encourage interaction between class members and recognition of various leadership behaviors
- To develop a broader perspective on leadership in every day circumstances

## Class Necessities:
- Student Workbooks
- 8 1/2" x 11" Designer paper *(paper with designs or borders on it. Available at various computer or office supply stores)*
- Markers and/or crayons
- Flip chart paper
- Masking tape

## Class Outline:

### Review Course Syllabus and Expectations:

Pass out student workbooks. Depending upon what your population is and what the set up of your course/program is, review appropriate syllabus and expectations. If you are using the Suggested Course Outline (in the back of this guide), spend time going over the organizational observation and paper requirements. You will want to revisit these in several class periods as well. In addition, you should set up your time line of dates for work to be turned in, as well as grading standards for your goals.

The Organizational Observation is designed to put the students in the position of evaluating a person's leadership behaviors as well as how their group responds to them. I have at times, had the student's write it as a letter to the leader (not to be sent!) so that they are serving as a leadership "consultant" and are offering frank feedback about the leader's strength and weaknesses.

Because this is the first meeting of the class, it is also important to conduct a relevant icebreaker for introductions prior to moving into the "defining leadership" stage of the class. Overall, this class period is a good opportunity to set the stage to challenge student's stereotypes of what a leader is and isn't, and to establish norms of the class.

### Icebreaker:

Pass out a piece of the designer paper to each student. Have a variety of markers and crayons available to entire class (put in middle of room or have them start with a few colors and trade with others).  Have the students place the piece of paper in front of them and to simply focus on it for a minute.  As they are looking at the sheet of paper, describe it as follows:

"In front of you is the most popular magazine selling on the newsstands 10 years from now.  The newsstands cannot keep this magazine in stock and everyone wants it.  On the cover is the most inspirational and successful person around.  The person on the cover is you.

Imagine why it is that you are on that cover.  What is the magazine's name?  What have you done to deserve such recognition?  (Examples: "Star Gazer Magazine — Javier Discovers New Comet!"; "Animals Today — Meet Renowned Veterinarian - Jennie Smith")"

Give them time to formulate and design their magazine "cover."  They do not have to be splendid artists to get their point across!  Also, be certain to have them include their name in the title or headline on the magazine front.  When all have completed, ask each student to stand up, introduce themselves, and explain their magazine cover.  Encourage the class to ask them additional questions about the cover and perhaps, the interests that it highlights.

## Defining Leadership Activity:

Following the icebreaker, transition into next activity.  Start by discussing, in general terms, that there are various ways to define leadership.  In fact, leadership research has come up with more than 4,000 definitions and they keep changing daily!  Talk about how people have different views on life and with that come different views on how they see leaders.  Encourage discussion and input from class.

Break class into groups of 3.  Encourage them to join up with new people (if they know others in the class).  On the "Defining Leadership Worksheet" in the workbook, have each small group brainstorm words and/or terms which come to mind when they think about leaders and/or leadership.  Discourage just listing names of leaders, rather they should list words which, good or bad, describe leadership qualities/characteristics.  You may need to define "Brainstorming" prior to them beginning so that they realize that brainstorming allows all thoughts to be put down, not only the terms with which everyone in the group agrees.

Once the small groups have completed their brainstorms, bring entire class back together.  Have small groups remain where they are.  One by one, have each group share their words/terms while you write them on the board or flip chart paper.  If you are using flip chart paper (recommended over using the chalkboard so that you can keep the list), it is helpful to take off three or four pieces and tape them to a wall or board so that all of the words can be seen at once.  In addition, if hung prior to the groups sharing their terms, it allows you to move quickly from one sheet to the next.  While each group is sharing their terms, the other groups should be placing check marks to the terms which are the same on their list.  By the end of the sharing, you should have a substantial list.  Encourage students to offer terms which are missing and should be added after all groups have shared.

I find it useful to type all of these words onto one master list to be passed out at next class session. If this is not feasible, it is helpful to write all words on newsprint so that they can be hung up at next class session.

## Debrief:

- How easy was it to come up with descriptive words?
- How many on the list can be seen as negative descriptors?
- What terms seemed to be similar for all groups?
- When you think of the people who are leaders in your life, how many of these terms describe them?
- What terms are unrealistic for us to expect in a leader? (Usually, terms such as "perfect" "flawless" "immortal in a way" are shared by one of the groups)
- How supportive and/or demanding are we of leaders to live up to some of these terms?
- How many of these terms describe you?
- How does it feel to live up to the terms listed?

## Reflection:  Page 5 or 6 (Alternate) of workbook.

Below list any and all words (good and bad) which come to mind when you think of "Leadership" or being a "Leader" (List words, not names of people who come to mind!):

_____

_____

_____

_____

_____

_____

_____

_____

_____

_____

# Characteristics of Leadership/Leaders (Good & Bad)

## *Sample Brainstorm List*

| | | | |
|---|---|---|---|
| Able to work under pressure | Able to take criticism | Ability to Debate | Ability to Make Decision |
| Accepting of Others | Active | Admired | Aggressive |
| Ambition | Anybody & Everybody | Any Race | Appreciative |
| Appropriate Goals | Articulate | Assertive | Attitude |
| Authority | Balanced | Beliefs | Believes in followers |
| Believes in self | Big-Headed | Calm | Caring |
| Challenging | Charisma | Choices | Committed |
| Common Sense | Communicates | Community | Companionship |
| Computer Literate | Conceited | Confident | Connections |
| Control (of Self & Group) | Cooperative | Courageous | Creativity |
| Dedicated | Delegates | Demands/Expectations | Dependable |
| Determined | Devoted | Dignity | Diligent |
| Direct | Disciplined | Discretion | Diverse/Brings Differences |
| Drug-Free | Dynamic | Eager | Easy Going |
| Easy to Communicate With | Educated | Egotistical | Emotional |
| Empathetic | Empowering | Encouraging | Energetic |
| Enthusiastic | Ethical | Example Setter | Faces Challenges |
| Fair-minded | Fearful | Financially-wise | Flexible |
| Focused | Followers | Forgiving | Friendly |
| Frank & Blunt | Futuristic | Glamorous | Goal Setting |
| Good-Follower | Good Self-Esteem | Guidance/Guiding | Hard Working |
| Has Opinions | Hazardous | Healthy | Helpful |
| Honest | Honorable | Human | Humble |
| Hypocritical | Ideas | Impartial | Independent |
| Influential | Initiative | Insensitive | Inspirational |
| Instinctive | Investigative | Jerk | Kind |
| Leap of Faith | Knowledge | Level-Headed | "Like a brother, sister, family" |
| Listener | Lots of Speeches | Loyal | Makes Mistakes |
| Mentally stable | Money | Morals, Principles, Values | Motivated |
| Motivational | Mutual Respect | Nationalistic Pride | Needs |
| No-Fear | Not a Hypocrite | Not always right | Open-Minded |
| Opinionated | Optimistic | Offensive | Organized |
| "Overpowerful" | Outgoing | Outspoken | Patient |
| Peaceful | People Person | People skills | Person in Command |
| Persuasive | Persistent | Popularity | Positive |
| Potential | Power | Powerful | Pride |
| Problem solver | Progressive | Promising | Public Speaker |
| Punctual | Punishable | Relates to others | Reliable |
| Representable | Respectable | Respects Constitutional Rights | Respects others |
| Responsible | Resourceful | Role Model | Roots & a Background |
| Sacrifice | Self-Respect | Self-Starter | Sense of Direction |
| Sensible | Sensitive | Skilled | Smart |
| Sophisticated | Straight Forward | Strength (Mental & Physical) | Strict/Has Standards |
| Strong Convictions | Strong Hearted | Strong-minded | Supportive |
| Sympathetic | Tactful | Takes Care of Self | Takes Charge |
| Talented | Teacher | Teamwork | Thinker |
| Thoughtful | Tolerant | Trustworthy/Trusting | Understanding |
| Understands Differences | Unique | Vision | Wise |
| Worthy | Willing to Accept Challenges | Willing to be outside the circle | Willing to be vulnerable |
| Words of Wisdom | Withstand pressure/stress | Willing to take on Responsibilities | Zealous/Spunky |
| Well-liked | Willing to deal with Consequences | Wants to Make a Difference | |

*Write below your personal definition of "leadership" and what it means to be a "leader." When people refer to you as a leader, what do you hope they are saying and/or thinking about you?*

_____

_____

_____

_____

_____

_____

_____

_____

_____

_____

_____

_____

_____

_____

_____

_____

_____

_____

*The man who lives by himself and for himself is apt to
be corrupted by the company he keeps.
~ Virginia Hutchinson*

### Goals:
- Continuing to define leadership in personal context
  - To differentiate between individuals who are leaders and the qualities or characteristics which make a person a leader
- Continuing to develop working relationships between students in class
- To challenge students to examine their expectations of leaders and to reflect on their abilities to meet these expectations for others

## Class Necessities:
- Student Workbooks
- Flip chart/Markers or Classroom Board /Chalk

## Class Outline:

As mentioned before, prior to class, I find it useful to type all of the words which the students brain stormed in previous class into one list. I then pass this out at the beginning of this class in order to focus and inspire discussion. If this is not feasible, hang up newsprint with comprehensive list of words from pervious class.

Introduce class topic by reflecting on personal leadership definitions developed from previous class.

### Ask students:
- Share your personal definition (from Reflection) and examples of when you saw your definition in action (either by yourself or others)?
- Are there any new terms came to mind since last class? What are they?
- How can some of these characteristics be identified? Especially ones which are a matter of opinion (words such as "dedicated"; "responsible"; "risk-taker"; "ethical"; etc. — use your judgment and encourage students to evaluate their lists)?
- Any other questions appropriate to your class dynamics and goals

To transition into first activity, discuss that the words on their lists describe general and overall CHARACTERISTICS of leaders and leadership. With all of these words, there are probably specific people who come to mind who possess or exhibit these characteristics or QUALITIES. The first class activity will focus on ten qualities which somewhat summarize what we look for in leaders (or that we should strive for if we want to be seen as a leader and/or held to leadership standards).

## Class Activity #1

### Ten Qualities of Leadership

Ask students to open their workbooks to the Ten Qualities of Leadership. Individually, they are to read through each description of the "Quality". As they are reading, they are to place the name of someone who comes to mind who clearly demonstrates this quality on the line beside the Quality. Encourage the students to think of a different person for each Quality.

It is helpful to have the students think of someone "well-known" so that others can relate to how others interpret each quality. In general, however, many will want to put the name of someone specific in their lives which is fine. Selecting people who are important in their lives also helps "localize" the issue of leadership and how every person has the potential to be a leader! (Good for discussion throughout the course!)

After your selected time (20 to 25 minutes is usually enough, depends upon reading level and analytic ability of students), bring class together to discuss and debrief. Read through or summarize each Quality and have students share any of the individuals who they thought of for each Quality.

### Wrap-up questions:
- Was easier or more difficult than the brainstorm from the previous class.
  In what way was it (easier) or (more difficult)?
- What similarities did the group have when individually defining each quality?
- What differences...?
- Other questions appropriate to your group...

(Take break or transition into next activity, as appropriate)

The next activity is designed to get the students to begin to reflect on themselves and their needs and expectations of leaders with regards to themselves. It is also designed to get the students comfortable with expressing their opinions with one another while focusing upon a goal.

## Class Activity #2

Now that you have spent time as a class defining leadership and identifying individuals who possess leadership qualities and thus are seen as Leaders (whether locally or globally), shift the attention of the class to focus on themselves — what they need from a leader (individually) and what makes a good leader (to the group).

Have all class members sit in a circle, with or without a table in center. Introduce page 10 of student handbook. Also, indicate that they are not to turn to the next page until instructed to do so, as a group. Give them approximately 5 minutes to complete page 10 individually.

Once all have completed, have each member share their results. You may want to keep a tally of the statements with the most "top 5" choices. After tallying, share your observations and ask for theirs (what did they hear from others? how many top 5 do they share? etc.)

Now have students turn to page 11. They are now to do a similar ranking, however this time, they must do it as an entire group. They may do it any way they want, as long as everyone is an active participant. As facilitator, you may need to encourage the "talkers" to listen and the "listeners" to talk! Suggest that they start with adding any missing characteristics from the list (on the blanks) prior to starting to rank. This time, they are to rank ALL of the statements.

This activity can take awhile, depending upon group dynamics. If you do not get to the point of discussion/debriefing, you may choose to complete that at next class session.

## Tips:
- If they get stuck early, you may want to encourage them to rank individually and then to work as a group
- It may be useful to offer suggestions on missing characteristics
  (if appropriate for your group)

## Debrief:

- What were the positives and negatives of the group process?
- What was it like to "give up" one of their high ranking characteristics?
- How many gave one up in order to keep another characteristic high on the list?
- What negotiations took place?
- Were certain roles/behaviors obvious (e.g. talking a lot or listening)?
- How do they work with others in a group where they do not feel contributions are equal?
- What did they learn is important for one another in the group? How will they use this information as the class goes on?
- Other questions relevant to the group?

Can someone be trained to become a leader? Can a person develop leadership abilities? Many say YES! Leadership is a combination of many personal qualities. It begins inside a person and relies both on philosophical approach and learned skills. Understanding the philosophy of leadership may come naturally or may be learned, and this knowledge distinguishes the leader from everyone else. Here are ten qualities of leadership which many people agree a leader should possess.

## Courage: _____

"Have the courage of your convictions" is a familiar saying. Leaders must have a strong belief system to meet leadership challenges and be able to maintain these beliefs. Believing in their own physical, emotional, intellectual, values, and spiritual standards allows them to apply their resources and creative energy when faced with problems or overwhelming odds. General George C. Patton said courage is "fear holding on another minute." Leaders are not swayed & "hold on." They venture forth with faith & stamina, setting an example others can follow.

## Big Thinker: _____

Leaders have the ability to see things in a larger perspective, and also to see things better than they are. Curiosity is essential. And many leaders have what Cavett Robert calls "divine discontent." They challenge tradition and the "status quo". They are not afraid of idealism and are eager to create and bring out the best in others. Leaders have clearly defined their personal goals and have the ability to help others expand their thinking and imagination.

## Change Master: _____

Leaders move people and things in directions more beneficial to all. Leaders not only have the ability to create change, but they also accept, handle, and succeed during times of change. Change is welcome since they learn from the past and let it go. Leaders don't burden themselves with old ideas, prejudices, habits, or processes. The inspired leader looks for opportunity in change and tries to understand it even if he or she doesn't like it. Leaders learn how to "accept things they cannot change, courage to change the things they can, and gain the wisdom to know the difference".

## Persistent and Realistic:

A leader sets realistic goals and sees them through to completion. Even under pressure, they remain committed to those goals. They can separate real and imaginary obstacles while recognizing the power of both. Current struggles are acknowledged as essential for future achievement, and leaders will sacrifice immediate satisfaction for future gains. Leaders have endurance and tenacity. They ignore distractions which will prevent completing a task or goal. They also help others overcome obstacles because they realize that patience is a good measure of persistence. Leaders do not quit.

## Sense of Humor:

It is said "If you take yourself too seriously, no one else will." A sense of humor is key. Leaders know that life and leading are no joking matter, but they have the ability to keep things in perspective. They are self-accepting. They have enthusiasm. Leaders are spontaneous and can express their feelings. Their wit and humor lightens the load of those with whom they associate. When stress and pressure become a problem, the leader's sense of humor gives everyone a momentary "emotional vacation" so that the task or situation can continue with balance and clear direction.

## Risk Takers:

Taking risks is important to leadership. Leaders have the courage to begin while others are waiting for better times, safer situations, and guaranteed results. They are willing to take a risk because they know that over-caution and indecision are robbers of opportunity and success. They are willing to fail in order to succeed. Leaders know that no one wins all the time, and winning is not always the goal. They take initiative, are independent, and are not unduly influenced by others. Leaders allow themselves and others to grow by making mistakes and not expecting unrealistic perfection.

## Positive and Hope-filled:

Eighty-percent of success in life is having a positive attitude. Leaders have the ability to see hope where others do not and to have faith when others give up. They know that one person with a belief is equal to 99 who only have an interest. They are optimistic and can get the same from others. They trust themselves and others. Leaders know that everyone wants to make a difference, accomplish something in life, be accepted, and receive recognition for their skills and talents. The leader takes action to reinforce a person's self-worth and value in a positive and hope-filled manner.

## Decision Maker:

Deciding to decide is often harder than carrying through once the decision has been made. Leaders know that not deciding is still a decision made by time, fate, and circumstances. Leaders are aware of this and would rather make the wrong decision than none at all. Few decisions in life are so critical that they cannot be corrected. Leaders know that indecision wastes time, energy, talent, money, and opportunity. They make decisions and commitments to avoid future failures. Leaders are also willing to make decisions and plans that affect future generations because they know that indecision may eliminate everyone's future.

## Accepts and Uses Power Wisely:

Leaders do not shrink from power, nor do they seek it unnecessarily. They know that having clout often intimidates others, so they use power carefully. They "pull rank" only in emergencies. Leaders use their power to direct others to help them achieve their full potential. Leaders take responsibility for themselves, their actions, and the results. They use their personal power to inspire this behavior in others. Power & greatness is not a goal, but a by-product of learning how to serve.

## Committed:

Commitment is the primary work for leaders. They realize that without it, all else is meaningless. They are excited and dedicated to their cause which pulls others to them. Their commitment exudes confidence and hope. Leaders set high standards of excellence for themselves and others, and people grow to meet those expectations.

Leaders determine a course, make a plan, and have self-discipline to follow through in spite of obstacles. Leaders stay in the game long after others give up. Most people quit too soon, missing the riches of life. Just like the seasons, life and leadership have cycles. A leaders commitment is sustained through the good & bad, hot & cold, ups & downs. Although leaders are committed to their goals, they live one day at a time and know that if they take care of today, tomorrow will take care of itself.

*Adapted from work by Sheila Murray Bethel*

## What Makes A Good Leader To You | Worksheet

*Study the list below.  Rank order — 1 being your first choice — the top FIVE actions which YOU believe a leader can take to be most effective in getting YOU to take part in a group's project.*

_____ 1. The leader would specifically explain my part in the project.

_____ 2. The leader would ask me personally about participating in the project.

_____ 3. The leader would show how I am needed.

_____ 4. The leader would give me a choice of tasks to perform in the project.

_____ 5. The leader would be friendly and kind to me.

_____ 6. The leader would explain the purpose of the project.

_____ 7. The leader would give me a part of the planning of the project.

_____ 8. The leader would keep me informed about what is going on.

_____ 9. The leader would be sold on the project.

_____ 10. The leader would seek my suggestions and listen to me.

_____ 11. The leader would give me background on the project.

_____ 12. The leader would treat me as an equal with them.

_____ 13. The leader would ask me first before others.

_____ 14. The leader would not criticize me, my ideas or performance in front of the rest of the group, and would talk with me in private about their concerns.

_____ 15. The leader would value the differences I bring to the organization & project.

_____ 16. The leader would "cut me some slack" if I need it, and if I made a mistake, would let it slide.

*Your task is to rank the following statements that describe the behavior of a good leader. Place a 1 in front of the statement that is the most important characteristic of an effective leader, place a 2 in front of the next most important characteristic, and so on. There may be some characteristics which are missing, so spend time thinking of those first and add them on the empty lines at the bottom of the list. You must work on this AS A GROUP. You may organize for work in any way that you wish as long as you work as a total group! Reach some kind of group decision on as many of the statements as you can.*

_____    1. Free with praise of work that is excellent in quality.

_____    2. Communicates the reason for all important decisions.

_____    3. Listens empathetically to complaints.

_____    4. Emphasizes informal working relationships (promotes social relationships) and does not only rely on "business" relationships to get things done

_____    5. Encourages criticism toward improving policies and procedures.

_____    6. Consults with others (both "above them" and "below them") before making decisions affecting them.

_____    7. Keeps cool under pressure and controls temper.

_____    8. Never reprimands or sanctions a person in front of others.

_____    9. Urges using channels in communicating with appropriate officials or decision makers beyond the group.

_____    10. Has regular meetings with others to discuss ways of improving working relationships.

_____    11. Works toward creating conditions in which the use of authority ("pulling rank") is rarely, if ever, needed.

_____    12. Values the diversity (differences) that people bring to the organization.

_____    13. Other characteristics which are necessary for a "good" leader:

_____        _____

_____        _____

*self assessment of leadership behaviors*

## Goals:
- To help students identify their strongest leadership behaviors
- To encourage interaction between class members & recognition of leadership behaviors
- To develop a leadership "philosophy" & ways to examine their leadership styles throughout the class and in their personal lives

## Class Necessities:
- Leadership Practices Inventory (LPI) - Self Student Form
  (or other youth-oriented leadership assessment tool)
- The Leadership Challenge handout
- LPI Interpretive Booklet
- Flip chart/Markers or Classroom board/Chalk

***All Leadership Challenge and Leadership Practices Inventory materials can be ordered from: Jossey-Bass Publishers 1-800-956-7739***

| | | | | | |
|---|---|---|---|---|---|
| G020 | LPI-Student Self | @ $2.50 | G089 | LPI-Facilitator's Package | @ $25.00 |
| G019 | LPI Student Workbook | @ $7.50 | | (includes guide, self inventory, & workbook) | |
| G018 | LPI-Facilitatoris Guide | @ $19.95 | G090 | Deluxe Facilitator's Pkg. | @ $35.00 |
| | | | | (same as above plus The Leadership Challenge book) | |

Jossey-Bass offers bulk order discounts when you order 10 or more of any item. The discount begins at 10% and goes up to 20% for orders of 100+. Allow 5-7 business days for your order.

I recommend that you purchase the facilitatoris guide or facilitator's package to have on hand. The guide provides background to the inventory as well as various ways to apply the information. After reviewing the guide, you may determine that you want to modify the following session plan with other activities highlighted in the guide.

## Class Outline:

### Introduce Styles of Leadership:

Have students brainstorm general characteristics of leadership styles —
Examples may include - dictator, democratic, powerful, motivating, etc.
Many of the words which were brain stormed in the first class can be incorporated here
Discuss how they take notice of different styles of leadership

### Introduce LPI:

Describe what the LPI is, how it was developed, for what it is used, etc. This is not a test with only one right answer! In fact, the LPI encourages people to look at themselves and what their behaviors and beliefs are about their own leadership style. If you are unfamiliar with the LPI, it is suggested that you read "The Leadership Challenge" by James Kouzes and Barry Posner.

Have students complete their LPI and tally on back page. The columns with the highest sum indicates the behavior in which the student most frequently engages. The columns should be totaled horizontally. At the bottom of each column, write the total for that column. Each column directly relates to one of the five behaviors. From left to right, the students can label the columns as follows:

(Column One)  Challenging The Process      (Column Two)  Inspiring a Shared Vision
(Column Three)  Enabling Others to Act      (Column Four)  Modeling the Way
(Column Five)  Encouraging the Heart

Describe five practices (put on flip chart or board - summarize definitions from "The Leadership Challenge" bi-fold)

- Challenging the Process    • Inspiring a Shared Vision    • Encouraging the Heart
- Enabling others to Act    • Modeling the Way

Ask students to give examples of these behaviors. Is it more comfortable in certain situations to behave a different way? How accurate is the LPI in describing your style/how you think you lead (and how others would say you lead)?

Go through first few pages of Booklet describing how reliable the LPI is; if people can change their behaviors, etc. Ask the students for feedback on how well their highest scoring area describes their style (whether as a leader or in everyday interactions with others, including family).

## Activity Option #1

Break into groups of three and conduct comparison pages in LPI booklet. Have members of each small group discuss with one another where their significant differences and similarities arise in each of the five behaviors.

After completion of comparison pages, have each group present what they discovered by sharing with others. Have group turn to the Action Pages for the LPI in the Appendix. There are six pages which highlight what "actions" they can take if they want to increase how they engage in any of the behaviors (one page has space for the students to brainstorm, either individually or together, on other actions). The actions can apply or be interpreted for individuals or for the group/team of which the students are members. They may decide to mark the actions they want to take and can include these in their reflection.Perhaps have them share the differences and similarities they found. When complete, assign reflection as stated following alternate activity below.

## Activity Option #2

Break into groups by the behavior which best describes each person. Typically, that is the score that was the highest for them, or the behavior which the student most naturally relates to as you go through the descriptions. Try to have groups split in a somewhat even fashion (that is, an equal number of students in each group). In their groups, have the students write on newsprint the characteristics which describe the behavior description to which they relate. They should include categories such as:

- With what type of people do you like best to work?
- What environment/attitude is most productive for you?
- Other than the LPI behavior description, what other terms would best describe a person in this group?

- How do others see you (in this behavior description)?
- What struggles do people face who practice this behavior the most?
- What other words describe your group?
- What would you like others to know about people who practice this behavior?
- Which other behavior does this group believe would be the best "marriage" of strengths/attitude?
- (Individually) What behavior do you wish you practiced more often?
- Other things which would help others understand your behavior description the best.

Once the groups have finished writing their responses and developing a more in-depth description of their most frequently practiced behavior, have each group present to the class. Provide time for others to ask questions of the group.

Once all groups have presented, have the students turn to the Action Pages for the LPI in the Appendix. There are six pages which highlight what "actions" they can take if they want to increase how they engage in any of the behaviors (one page has space for the students to brainstorm, either individually or together, on other actions). The actions can apply or be interpreted for individuals or for the group/team of which the students are members. They may decide to mark the actions they want to take and can include these in their reflection. There is also a Leadership Action Plan page which you may choose to use as the reflection assignment if you do not purchase the interpretive booklets.

Assign reflection pages in the interpretive booklet (pages 13 &14) or use the Leadership Action Plan from the Appendix. Encourage the students to focus their goal/action plan in terms of leadership behaviors, not necessarily just setting any goal. This is a good time for them to include the actions they marked on the pages in the appendix.

**Reflection:**     Pages 13 and 14 of LPI Booklet or Leadership Action Plan (in Appendix)

## Goals:
• To demonstrate the differences of people as leaders as well as differentiate group members
• To discuss human behavior and how leaders can impact that behavior, both positively and negatively
• To understand McGregor's theories of human behavior
• To discuss types and the impact of power, positive and negative
• To discuss differences and relationship between authority, influence, and power

## Class Necessities:
• Student Workbooks
• Set of Fiddlestix® (or Tinker Toys®)
• Two copies of Leadership Skit outline for Leaders #1 and #2 (in facilitators guide)
• Copy of Fiddlestix® Construction outline (in facilitators guide)
• Flip chart/Markers or Classroom Board /Chalk

If you use Tinker Toys® for this activity, the color references included will need to be checked to determine if there are enough pieces for four participants to complete the projects. You may modify these directions as necessary for the number of construction pieces available for four people. In addition, wooden Tinker Toys® are recommended over the plastic ones, although they are no longer available at toy stores. Fiddlestix® are available at educational toy stores and other toy outlets.

## Class Outline:

### Class Activity:

Ask for two volunteers to serve as leaders for the class activity. For the rest of the class, ask for five volunteers to be the "organization" for the leaders. They should move to the center of the classroom, sitting around a table. The rest of the class members should serve as observers.

Take the two leader volunteers just outside of the room and hand them their instructions. Indicate that they must take on the part they select and should respond to the group in that role. One should be Leader #1 and the other shall be Leader #2. You may chose to have two students volunteer prior to class to be the leaders; in that case, give them their instructions prior to class (tell them not to share their roles with others in the class!).

Leader #1 is to be "group-centered"; being interactive with the group yet still maintaining her/his role as a leader. This leader should guide the group to work cooperatively on their Fiddlesticks® projects and should encourage each group member.

Leader #2 is to be "leader-centered"; directive and authoritative to the group. The structure of the group is more important to this leader than is the creativity of their projects. This leader should pick a favorite in the group who can do no wrong, while sacrificing other relationships with the group. This leader's motto is "My way or the highway" and feels that s/he is the one who knows best. The directions that Leader #2 has the group follow are purposely vague. Address this issue during debriefing.

You may need to prompt the students into their role when they reenter the class and begin the activity. Encourage and support their role playing yet do not interfere with the activity in process.

## Debrief:

### Once the activity is completed, pull the entire group together to discuss:

• What happened in the first group?  second group?

• What was it like to be a member of the first group?  second group?

• How did the leaders respond to each other?

• Which did you prefer? (ask each member of the group as well as observers)

• What could be the positives and negatives of Leader #1?

• What could be the positives and negatives of Leader #2?

• How did it feel to be the favorite?

• How did it feel to be the one who was asked to leave? (possibly for no apparent reason!)

• (To the leaders) Was your behavior natural or unnatural for you?  What is similar and/or different?

• Ask observers what they observed?

• What role did power play in this activity?

• Other questions relevant to your group?

## Lecturette:

Have students turn to Human Behavior Worksheet in the student workbook.
Go through the next two pages, slowly and as a group.  Relate McGregor's theories to the activity.

Differentiate between the Leader's behaviors and the members of the groups.
McGregor's theories relate to the members of the groups, that is:

• Leader #1 believed that his/her group members were capable and self motivated and needed very little  direction — they were seen as "Y People"
• Leader #2 believed that his/her group members were not capable and self-motivated, needed a lot of structure,  and needed to be told what to do — they were seen as "X People"

The leaders were neither X nor Y, rather they were "Group-Centered" (Leader #1) or "Leader-Centered" (Leader #2) (on page 12 there is an area to brainstorm these different types of leadership...have the students brainstorm as a class, giving examples)

Group-Centered Leadership depends heavily on the contributions of the group, with the leader often serving as "facilitator" or for subtle guidance.

Leader-Centered Leadership is much more directive and generally sounds like "My way or the highway" when coming from the leader.

Define the three "technical" approaches to leadership as shown on the Continuum. "Abdicrat" is where there is no leader and the group makes all decisions together. "Democrat" is where each person has a voice/vote and the leader makes decisions from this. "Autocrat" is where the leader makes all decisions. You may want to provide examples.

Many times, the students will want to say that the leaders are either X or Y, when in fact, McGregor's theory relates to how leaders treat the people in their organizations in order to get things done.

Discuss, as a class, how people tend to be a combination of these types, depending upon the situation in which they are in. For example, when an individual is very excited and motivated by what they are doing, they will not necessarily need a lot of direction or structure. In other situations, people will like to be told what to do and how to do it. This is especially true if a very particular outcome is expected of the leader.

Both types of leaders are able to accomplish certain things based upon the POWER they have with their group.

Review Types of Power in student workbook and how it relates to leadership styles and with members of a group. Read through each type of power; have students give an example of how each type of Power can be used in a POSITIVE and in a NEGATIVE way.

## *You may need to give examples:*

**Reward Power** — e.g. While shopping at the grocery store, a father promises his daughter a candy bar if she will be quiet until they are done
• Positive - it motivates the daughter to be quiet
•Negative - once the daughter figures it out, she will only be quiet if she gets candy

**Referent Power** — e.g. Peer pressure can inspire someone to do well academically, especially if a friend they admire encourages them to do well
• Positive - doing well academically
• Negative - Peer pressure can also inspire someone to make poor choices if that same friend is acting up

**Legitimate Power** — e.g. The President of the United States; Police; Teachers/Principal
• Positive - while that person holds position, we respect and respond to them in that position
• Negative - if that person were not in position, they may or may not have power with us

**Information Power** — e.g. The secretary to a leader of a business or organization
- Positive — that person can schedule meetings with leaders of organization and can answer questions as necessary
- Negative — that person can prevent information from getting through to leaders or can keep people from getting to meet the leader

**Expert Power** — e.g. Doctors; Lawyers; Expert Witnesses in court cases
- Positive — they can give us the best and most accurate information
- Negative — we may trust them too much and they could take advantage of us

**Connection Power** — e.g. Knowing people in high places or people who can get things done
- Positive — knowing someone who can help you get a job or get into a special school
- Negative — not knowing someone and being kept out of certain jobs or schools

**Coercive Power** — e.g. Directive leaders who make you do something you do not want to do
- Positive — sometimes it is the only way to get things done (the concept of "tough love")
- Negative — most of the time, coercive power IS negative!  Sexual harassment; firing people for no apparent reason if they don't do something; penalizing students with bad grades, etc.

Discuss the impact of Power in society and how they as leaders would like to use power. Connect discussion to activity and to McGregor's theories.  In addition, you may like to have a free flow discussion on issues of power in the lives of the students.  My experience has been that these are enlightening and productive discussions (as long as they are moderated — especially with regards to the police or other similar authority figures!).  It is helpful to discuss how power can be used to do very good things in society and what roles leaders can take to "use power wisely."

After this discussion, review Authority and Influence, particularly noting the subtleties of the two concepts..  It is helpful to keep Power as part of this discussion.  Discuss how each of these (Power, Influence, and Authority) exist in each of the student's lives.  It may be helpful to put all three words on the chalkboard and have the students brainstorm examples of each. This discussion will result in lively debate on how each student defines the words.  It is important to point out that we may define words differently depending upon our frame of reference and personal experiences.  This is especially true when putting the three words into action.

Bring class to appropriate closure.  You may or may not get through all of material for this module in one class period.  If not, continue at the next session.

## Reflection:

Pages 16 or 17 (Alternate) of workbook

# Instructions - Fiddlestix® Activity
## (make copies for the two leaders)

## Leader Number One:

Leader Number One empties the Fiddlestix® onto the table and gives the group the following instructions:

• The group may build anything they want with the Fiddlestix®.

• You may build individually or as a group.

• You can move around the table and interact with the others as much as you want.

• You may speak, laugh, and in general, communicate with one another.

• You will have about ten minutes to make your creations.

It is very important that Leader Number One create an open, comfortable climate during this part of the activity. You can move around and interact with the group as well. Make sure you give them a lot of praise and positive feedback. Ask them what they are making and engage in conversations with the group.

After about ten minutes, Leader Number One should ask them to explain what they have made for their final creation. Group members should be encouraged to be creative and explain anything they think is important about their creation.

## *Just after this part is completed....ENTER LEADER NUMBER TWO!!!!*

## Leader Number Two:

Leader Number two should break into the conversation abruptly. S/he should say that the projects they just made are dumb and that the leader did it all wrong from what they had talked about doing. Leader Number Two should be very different from Number One and should put down the first leader while s/he tells the group to take apart their projects. S/he should say things like "you did it all wrong"; "I can't believe that you think this is creative, all it was is chaos!"; "I thought we agreed that we would keep it very organized"

This leader should be very directive and authoritative.

Once Leader Number Two has had the group take their projects apart to start over (or has taken them apart themselves!), s/he should give them the following instructions:

(Leader # 2 continued)

- The members must each sit right next to the table and have their own space.
- There is to be NO TALKING with each other.
- If anyone has a question, they are to raise their hand and be acknowledged by the leader before speaking.
- Each member is to work on his/her own project.

The leader will take the members step-by-step through the Instruction sheet (attached). During the activity, Leader Number Two should be as authoritative as possible and should deal harshly with anyone who makes a mistake, fails to follow directions, or talks or giggles.

The leader should also select one person throughout the process to give praise (sometimes at the expense of others being put down and compared to this other person!).  At about the fifth instruction, the leader should randomly ask someone to leave the group, supposedly because they are doing something "wrong" or just aren't right for the group!

At the end of what the members have built, Leader Number Two should make them tell him/her, one at a time, what they have built.

# Directions For Fiddlesticks® Construction

## Give these instructions to Leader #2
(Use these instructions with no more than four participants if using 90 piece Fiddlesticks®)

1. Pick up the large round disc with the hole in the center and holes around the rim.

2. Pick up the long red stick and insert it in the hole in the center of the disc.

3. Pick up another round disc with the hole in the center and holes around the rim.

4. Insert the red stick into one of the holes in the rim of the disc.

5. Pick up a blue stick and insert into the hole on the right side of the rim of the disc.

6. Pick up another blue stick and insert it into the hole on the left side of the rim of the disc.

*(Leader #2 should randomly ask one of the group members to leave; say that the person is not following along, or is not quick enough, or is just not good enough, etc.)*

7. Pick up an orange stick and insert it into the hole at the top rim of the disc.

8. Pick up another round disc with the hole in the center and holes around the rim. Attach the disc to the orange stick by inserting the orange stick into one of the holes on the rim of the disc.

10. Pick up a green stick and attach it to the disc by inserting it into the hole on the rim opposite from the orange stick.

11. Pick up a blue stick and insert it into the hole on the rim of the disc immediately to the right of the orange stick.

12. Pick up another round disc with the hole in the center and holes around the rim. Attach it to the blue stick by inserting the stick into one of the holes on the rim of the disc.

14. Pick up a yellow stick and attach it to the disc by inserting it into the hole immediately to the left of the green stick.

15. Pick up a round ball with a hole in the center and holes around the rim.

16. Attach the ball to the yellow stick by inserting the stick into one of the holes on the rim of the ball.

17. Pick up a yellow stick and attach it to the ball in the hole directly opposite the yellow stick which has  already been attached on the left side of the green stick.

18. Pick up a yellow stick and attach it to the disc in the hole directly opposite the blue stick which has already been attached to the right side of the orange stick.

19. Pick up a wooden button end with a hole in only one end.

20. Attach the green stick to the wooden button end by inserting the stick into the hole.

# Douglas McGregor's Theory About Human Behavior

Human behavior is based on theory — that is, if we do "A" we theorize that it makes "B" will happen. It is important that a leader know his/her assumptions and theory about what makes people behave as they do. The leader's beliefs reflect their value system & also help determine how they practice and how they approach decision making & action.

Douglas McGregor, in The Human Side of Enterprise, developed two theories about human behavior:

- **Theory X** builds on the lower order of human needs and motivations
  (that is, pretty basic things motivate these people).

- **Theory Y** assumes that, once met, these lower needs no longer motivate.
  This builds on the higher human needs.

These are ways of looking at people who are members of your organization, not necessarily what type of leader a person is. Each type of person, (X or Y), may work better with different types of leaders. This isn't to say that only one type of leader works well with an X or a Y person, it is just helpful to understand what motivates people in your organization or group before you lead in just one way.

## Theory X (or "X people") believes:
- The average person has a natural dislike of work and will avoid it if possible;
- Because these type of people dislike work, most people must be coerced, controlled, directed, and/or threatened with punishment to get them to put forth effort toward the achievement of organizational goals;
- The average person being prefers to be directed, wishes to avoid responsibility, has little ambition, and wants "security" above all.

## Theory Y (or "Y people") believes:
- Putting energy into work is as natural as play or rest;
- The threat of punishment is not the only way to bring about effort toward organizational goals. People will be self-directed & show self-control in reaching goals to which s/he is committed;
- Commitment to goals is related to the rewards associated with achievement;
- People learn (under the right conditions) to accept and seek responsibility ;
- Being able to explore and express your imagination is an ability that nearly everyone possesses.

Leaders and group members should not choose "sides" as to which theory is "right" but should be certain to know how they look at other individuals and their own behavior. Theory Y is more dynamic than X, more optimistic about the possibility for human growth and development, and more concerned with self-direction and self-responsibility. Theory X fits more specifically to people who need others to motivate them, desire structure, and can work within an organization where decisions come from the top level only.

Theory X or Theory Y influence how leaders plan for decision making and action.

## If we accept Theory X (type of people in a group), then it would make sense to have:
- One way communication
- Strategy planning by the top leaders only
- Decision-making at the top level only
- A handing down of decisions to be implemented by the middle and lower level people
- A handing down of instructions to be carried out by lower levels
  (nothing goes up except reports!)

## Theory Y (type of people in a group) would want to have:
- Two way communication
- Involvement in goal setting, planning, and decision making at each level
- Responsibilities and instructions shared throughout organization

........................................................................................

## Continuum of Leadership
**(people generally fall somewhere in the middle):**


"Abdicrat"                          "Democrat"                          "Autocrat"
_____


*Group-Centered Leadership:*




*Leader-Centered Leadership:*

**Reward Power:**
Based on the leader's ability to provide rewards and positive consequences  based on compliance  (such as pay, promotions, recognition).

**Referent Power:**
Based on people liking the leader personally and are therefore willing to do things because of  their admiration for the leader.

**Legitimate Power:**
Based on a position held by the leader which people believe gives the leader authority.

**Information Power:**
Based on the leader's possession of or access to information that is perceived as valuable.

**Expert Power:**
Based on the leader's possession of expertise, skill, and knowledge, which through respect,  influences others.

**Connection Power:**
Based on the leader's "connections" with influential or important people inside or outside  the organization.

**Coercive Power:**
Based on fear, with the leader having the ability to remove positive consequences, administer  sanctions, and punish those who do not cooperate.

## AUTHORITY

1. Authority is the Power to act or command, to give orders and to see that they are carried out.

2. Authority can be GIVEN to a person by someone else or by an organization and it can be TAKEN AWAY.

3. Authority belongs to the POSITION, the rank (think of the President) and NOT to the PERSON who happens to occupy the position or hold the rank.

4. Authority gives ORDERS.

5. Authority produces COMPLIANCE regardless of consent or agreement.

6. Authority depends upon FORCE.

7. Authority DEMANDS, pushes.

8. Authority is ONE-PERSON rule.

9. Authority generates RESISTANCE.

10. Authority says GO - DO FOR ME.

11. Authority wants ITS plan fulfilled.

12. Authority is rule from ABOVE.

13. Authority offers NO CHOICE.

## INFLUENCE

1. Influence on the other hand is a HUMAN QUALITY; an ability to produce an effect in human behavior.

2. Influence is a quality BORN into every human being and no one else can give it to you are ever take it away.

3. Influence belongs to the PERSON individually for all time.

4. Influence makes SUGGESTIONS.

5. Influence generates willing cooperation, CONSENT and agreement.

6. Influence depends upon REASON AND LOGIC.

7. While influence LEADS.

8. Influence is DEMOCRACY - "we" in action.

9. While influence generates COOPERATION.

10. Influence says COME (join me).

11. Influence suggests OUR plans be accomplished.

12. Influence rules WITH its followers on their level.

13. While influence DOES.

*Adapted from "You Can Be A Leader" by Ben Soloman*

*Reflect on the various things that we did today - the Fiddlesticks activity with leaders who treated the group like Y-people & then like X-people; the continuum of leadership styles; and Types of Power. Select one (or more) of the following and write your thoughts on the topic:*

• *How do you think you treat people in groups (as Xs or Ys), and what happens in a group by how you treat them?*

• *How would you describe yourself on the continuum of leadership...as "group-centered"' or as "leader-centered" or as a combination, and why?*

• *Select one (or more) of the types of power and explain how they can be used in a positive and negative way.*

_____

_____

_____

_____

_____

_____

_____

_____

_____

_____

_____

_____

_____

*You can't take sides when you know the earth is round.*
*~ Patricia Sun*

### Goals:
- To introduce students to communication styles and skills
- To promote communication within group
- To continue building group identity and team
- To explore communication and listening as necessary skills for leaders

## Class Necessities:
- Student workbook
- Open classroom or area (push all desks/tables & chairs to side of room)
- 16 or more balls/round items of various sizes and textures (rubber and plastic balls; small stuffed animals, bean bags; foam balls are not as useful unless they have some weight to them; do not use tennis balls or anything harder! All balls/items should be the size of softballs and smaller) I find it useful to collect balls and "stuff" as I see them, and keep them in a 5 gallon paint tub
- Digital stopwatch or wristwatch with start/stop
- "New Story" story line

## Class Outline:

You may choose to replace, insert, or supplement any of the activities for this class session. There are numerous GREAT activities which accomplish similar communication and listening goals as the activities included here. Strong resources for communication and team building activities include (all resource information is listed in back of guide):

- Project Adventure, Inc.
- Silver Bullets: A guide to initiative problems, adventure games and trust activities by Karl Rohnke
- Cowstails and Cobras II: A guide to games, initiatives, ropes courses, and adventure curriculum by Karl Rohnke
- The Encyclopedia of Icebreakers: Structured activities that warm up, motivate, challenge, acquaint and energize by Sue Forbess-Greene

## Class Activities:

### Sequence of Activities:
- Group Juggle/Warp Speed
- Birthday Line Up
- Circle Count
- News Story ("Rumor Clinic")

## Description of Activities:

### Group Juggle/Warp Speed

This activity is a classic in terms of getting groups to work together, focus on a goal, and actively communicate with one another. This activity also uses all aspects of communication senses — speaking, listening, seeing, acting. There are various ways of doing this activity. I prefer to begin the activity with one ball circling the group and ending the activity with a number of balls equal to the number of people in the group.

Have the students form a circle, all standing up, and no chairs in the way or being used. Introduce the activity by remarking that the group is a "friendly" group, and with that it means that they openly communicate with each other by stating one another's name when tossing the ball to each other, both for obvious reasons (!) and to reinforce knowing names. Their first goal is to set up a group pattern in tossing one ball around the circle. The few rules that apply include:

- The ball must be tossed to someone who is not directly next to the person tossing;
- Each person must catch and throw the ball only once;
- The last person to catch the ball cannot be the first person tossing the ball;
- The ball must remain in the air (i.e. bouncing it once is not appropriate);
- People should state the person's name prior to tossing (!);
- People should be aware of where they are tossing the ball (safety factor).

Once the group has established their ball pattern, indicate that you are now going to time them with that one ball. Time them a first time. The second time, ask them to set a group goal of the time it will take to get the ball around. Once they have completed the task with one ball, indicate that you believe they are capable of adding more balls, up to the number of people in the group. They will be hesitant! Therefore, begin this phase of the activity by having them state how many balls they want to add to the "juggling" pattern. Again, they are to keep the same pattern, just adding more balls. Each time they establish the number of balls, have them successfully complete the pattern once, and then time them at least once. Continue this process until they end on a successful note and have added a significant number of balls.

## Debrief:

**Have the group discuss their successes and failures with this activity. Questions may include:**

- What was necessary for the group to succeed?

- How did you feel if you dropped the ball and stopped the pattern? How did the group feel?

- What was important in terms of communicating with each other?

- How long did it take for everyone in the group to realize their part/role?
- What happened if someone had difficulty catching (or tossing) consistently? How did the group help?
- What impact did timing your pattern have on the group? On individuals?
- How can you apply this activity to real life and leadership?
- Other questions relevant to your group's experience.

## Birthday Line Up Activity:

There are also a variety of ways to do this activity.  In general, the goal of this activity is also to have the group accomplish a goal which relies on all members.  The difference is that they "lose" their communication sense of speaking and must conduct this activity silently.

Set up the activity by mentioning that you will give them instruction for their goal.  Once you have given them instructions, they may ask questions of you for clarification but they may not strategize nor speak with one another.  In addition, tell them that they are to complete the goal without verbally communicating with one another, nor using any other resources around the room or on their body (i.e. calendars, student ID, driver's licenses, paper and pen, etc.).

The goal of the activity is for the group to line themselves up in order of birthdays — by month and day.  When the group believes they are done, they are to raise their hands.  Not until everyone in the group has raised their hand should you consider them done.

## Debrief:
- What was necessary for the group to succeed?
- What methods came up for you to communicate with one another without speaking?
- When you were first given your instructions, what did you think?
- How did people begin to know what to do?
- Was there a common "language" which developed?
- What would have happened if these were the same instructions you were given by a leader when working on  a difficult project?
- How long did it take for everyone to realize their role, direction, etc.?
- How can you apply this activity to real life and leadership?
- Other questions relevant to your group's experience.

## News Story Activity:

*(have four students volunteer to participate; all others should observe what occurs)*

Have the one of the first volunteers stay in the room. All of the others should be sent to a non-disruptive location where they cannot hear or see what is happening in the class room. Prepare the first volunteer only by stating that they must pay attention to what you are about to tell them. Remind observers that they are to be silent and to take note of what occurs.

**Tell Volunteer #1 that s/he has been a witness to a terrible accident.**
**Tell her/him the details:**

> A red BMW was driving (North/South/East/West) on (Local Street Name) at noon on (Day) when a large St. Bernard dog ran across the lawn of a blue house and into the street in hot pursuit of a Frisbee. The driver slammed on the brakes, sending the car into a 180 degree spin in front of oncoming traffic. The tail of the BMW smashed into a silver 1973 Subaru station wagon. The driver of the station wagon was a 50 year old man with two poodles in the front seat. When pedestrians assisted the man from the vehicle, the poodles leaped out and ran after the St. Bernard. The man fainted in the center turn lane and an ambulance was called. One of the poodles suffered minor bite injuries on the right leg but the other was fatally injured by a passing Harley-Davidson. Two (your school name) students playing Frisbee at the time of the accident, swear that the driver of the red car was in excess of the 35 mile per hour speed limit.

• After telling the story, tell the student that as witness to this accident, s/he must tell a Police Officer EXACTLY what happened. At this point, bring volunteer #2 into the room and tell her/him that s/he is a police officer who has arrived at the scene of this accident and will be told details of what happened. Volunteer #1 tells story.

• After Volunteer #2 (Police Officer)has been told the story, tell Volunteer #2 that s/he must repeat the details to the medical personnel who arrive on the scene. At this point, bring volunteer #3 into the room and tell her/him that s/he is a paramedic who has arrived on the scene of this accident and will be told details of what happened. Volunteer #2 tells story.

• After Volunteer #3 (Paramedic) has heard details, tell Volunteer #3 that s/he must repeat the details to the news reporter who is preparing for the six o'clock broadcast. At this point, bring Volunteer #4 into the room and tell her/him that s/he is a news reporter gathering information about an accident for the broadcast. Volunteer #3 tells story.

• After Volunteer #4 (News Reporter) has heard details, tell Volunteer #4 that s/he must report the details for the broadcast. Watching the broadcast is the son/daughter of the 50 year old man who was injured. At this point, bring last volunteer into room and tell her/him that s/he are watching the news for more information on the accident in which his/her father was in.  Volunteer #4 tells story.

When all players have completed their version of the story, repeat the true story for all to hear.

## Debrief:

- What happened to the translation of events?
- How does this happen in real life?
- If you are leading an organization or making a decision, and you do not check out your facts, what can happen?
- What were the observers thinking as you heard the story lose its "facts"?
- What is the impact of rumor, gossip, or modifying information on a group?
- What role do you (as an individual) usually play in these types of situations?  Is it helpful or harmful?
- How can you apply this activity to real life and leadership?
- Other questions relevant to your group's experience.

Once you have completed all of the activities, review as a group, the pages in student workbook on Communication and Listening, Active Listening, Non-Verbal Communication, and Feedback.  Pay particular attention to the Non-Verbal Communication sheet, as many youth are not as aware of the impact of their non-verbals to the context of their verbal communication.

## Reflection:   Communication Quiz (page 24) and Page 25 or 26 (Alternate).

Active listening is the ability to listen effectively to another person with whom we are having a discussion. Before we can effectively use active listening, we need to become more aware of some of the activities we normally do instead of listening. Things that interfere with our ability to listen are called "LISTENING BLOCKS." Review the blocks below and see which ones you use to avoid listening, and which ones others are using to avoid listening to you!

## LISTENING BLOCKS

### Rehearsing

You don't have time to listen when you are rehearsing what to say next. Your whole attention is on the design and preparation of your next comment. You have to look interested, but your mind is going a mile a minute because you are thinking about what to say next. Some people rehears entire chains of responses: "I'll say, then he'll say, " and so on.

### Judging

If you prejudge someone as stupid or incompetent or uninformed, you don't pay much attention to what the other person has said. You have already written them off. Hastily judging someone or something as wrong, inaccurate, outdated or unimportant means you have stopped listening and have begun a "knee-jerk" reaction. A basic rule of listening is that judgments should be made only after you have heard and evaluated the content of the message.

### Identifying

In this block, you take everything a person tells you and relate it back to your own experience. They want to tell you about a toothache and that reminds you of the time you had oral surgery for receding gums! You launch into your story before they can finish theirs. Everything you hear is utilized as a platform from which you tell some related story. You are so busy with these exciting tales of your life that there is not time to really hear the other person!

### Advising

You are the great problem-solver, ready with help and suggestions. You don't have to hear more than a few sentences before you begin searching for the right advice. However, while you are coming up with suggestions and convincing someone to "just try it," you may miss what is most important. You have just given advice for a problem you have not fully understood! At best, people feel unlistened to by you; at worst, you push them to implement a solution that is inappropriate.

### Sparring or Battling

This block has you arguing and debating with people. The other person never feels heard because you are so quick to disagree. In fact, a lot of your focus is on finding things with

*Mariam MacGregor, Copyright © 2000*

which to disagree. You take strong stands and are very rigid about your beliefs and preferences. The way to avoid sparring is to repeat back and acknowledge what you have heard. Try to look for one thing with which you might agree.

### Put-Downs

This is a type of sparring. This is when you use cutting or sarcastic remarks to put-down the other person's point of view. The put-down is effective for pushing communication into stereotyped patterns in which each person repeats familiar hostile statements.

### Being Right

Being right means you will go to great lengths (that is, try to twist the facts, start shouting, make excuses or accusations, calling up past "sins", etc.) to avoid being wrong. You can't listen to criticism, you can't be corrected, and you can't take suggestions to change. Your convictions and beliefs are unshakable, and since you will not acknowledge that your mistakes are mistakes, you just keep making them!

### Derailing

This listening block is accomplished by suddenly changing the subject. You derail the train of conversation when you get bored or uncomfortable with a topic. Another way of derailing is by joking it off. This means that you continually respond to whatever is said with a joke in order to avoid the discomfort or anxiety of seriously listening to the other person.

### Smoothing Over

"Right...right...absolutely...I know...Of course you are...Yes...Really?" You want to be nice, pleasant, supportive and you want people to like you. Therefore, you tend to agree with everyone to prevent tension or upset. You may half-listen, just enough to get the drift, but you are not really involved. You are placating (smoothing over) rather than tuning in and really listening to what is being said.

### Dreaming

When we dream, we pretend to listen but really tune the other person out while we drift about in our interior fantasies. Instead of disciplining ourselves to truly concentrate on the input, we "turn the channel" to a more entertaining subject!

Active listening is the most powerful communication tool of all.  When we stop talking or thinking and begin to truly listen supportively to others, all interaction becomes easier and less stressful.

## *Active listening does the following:*

### • It encourages and reinforces the speaker
Active listening not only encourages the other person to speak further; it reinforces your relationship with the speaker.

### • It feeds back your interpretations of the message
Active listening assures you have understood the other person correctly and invites them to expand on what they are saying without having to think of another question.

### • It probes for deeper, more sensitive comments
Often the information you really need is the most risky and is not readily disclosed.  Active listening can pull out that sensitive data that lurk below the surface.

### • It brings up unspoken feelings
Often such unspoken feelings form a serious obstacle to moving ahead.  Active listening can help move feelings along sot that you can solve the business problem.

### • Facilitates and guides the other person in their thoughts
In other words, sometimes our listening actually helps the other person to clarify his/her thinking.  When we are actively engaged in listening to the other person, they begin to realize how important it is for them to speak clearly and express their information clearly as well.

## How To Listen Actively

### *Prodding*
This describes the behaviors that gently reinforce the listener and prod them to further disclose.  Eye contact, facial expressions, body posture, nodding the head saying "I see.." or "Uh Huh..." are all examples of prodding.

### *Probing*
Probing digs deeper.  If someone says, "I don't think that will work for me," probing asks them "Why."  Probes can be very powerful and should be asked gently and unaggressively.

## Basic probes include:

How so?   Tell me more...   In what way?   How's that?   In what sense?

## Paraphrasing
This describes feeding back your interpretation of the speaker's message for verification and correction. It increases the likelihood that you have understood the speaker and show him/her that you understand how they are thinking. Another form of paraphrasing is summarizing in which you summarize the key points in your discussion to assure the listener that you understand. It also helps keep both the listener and speaker on track.

## Echoing
Echoing is simply repeating a key word or phrase in a gently, questioning tone in order to invite the speaker to expand. This tool can be used with probes.

## Reflecting
This connects you to the emotional messages which are implied in what the other person says:

• Sounds like you are upset...
• Sounds like you are overwhelmed...
• I sense that you disagree...

## Acknowledging
To acknowledge means to let the other person know you understand the other person's thoughts and feelings in an accepting, understanding, and non-judgmental way. Often this is what people need the most of in order to put aside bad feelings and get on with solving problems. "You feel angry because I didn't show up for our appointment...I can understand that, I know how busy you've been..." Notice that acknowledging does not necessarily imply agreeing!

Our bodies, eyes and faces are always providing non-verbal communication to both the listener and the speaker. In addition, how well our message is received is often measured by the non-verbal responses. The messages sent and the messages received are much more than the words used in sending the message.

## *There are five parts to non-verbal communication:*

**POSTURE:**
Standing above someone who is sitting can suggest dominance; leaning forward can suggest interest; slouching can suggest boredom, etc.

**GESTURES:**
Gestures compliment the verbal message. A clenched fist often suggests anger; a pointed finger can suggest dominance; fidgety hands suggest nervousness.

**EYE CONTACT:**
Eye contact controls the listening/attention and behavior of the listener. Staring suggests dominance or anger; avoiding eye contact can suggest submission; looking downward suggests shame, etc.

**FACIAL EXPRESSIONS:**
Facial expressions are often used in an attempt to mask the true intent of the message (example: smiling when angry). It is important to be certain that facial expressions are consistent with the message.

**VOCAL QUALITIES:**
What we say can be dramatically changed by how our voice that are used when the message is presented. The qualities include: volume (how loud), pitch (how high), quality and articulation (how clear). These qualities often give away the true meaning of what we are saying.

**WARNING!!!** An important thing to remember is that non-verbal communication can be strongly connected to culture and gender. If a person does not look at you or uses unknown gestures, investigate their culture by asking, rather than assuming that they aren't listening or interested in communicating.

Feedback has certain key ingredients: caring, trusting, acceptance, openness, and a concern for the needs of others.  When asking for feedback, the individual is asking for others' perceptions and feelings about his/her behavior.  Feedback is to be descriptive, non-evaluative, specific, and should embody freedom of choice.

## *Guidelines for helpful feedback:*

1.  Give feedback that is intended to help.

2.  Focus feedback on the behavior rather than the person. (The person will be less likely to become defensive.)

3.  Focus feedback on descriptions rather than judgments.

4.  Focus feedback on descriptions of behavior which are in terms of "more or less" rather than in terms of "either-or."

5.  Focus feedback on behavior related to a specific situation, preferably to the "here and now," rather than on behavior in the abstract, placing it in the "there and then" (i.e. bringing up the past).

6.  Focus feedback on the sharing of ideas and information rather than on giving advice. (This is very important because the individual needs to make his/her own decisions on what to do and how to move forward).

7.  Focus feedback on exploring alternatives rather than answers or solutions.

8.  Focus feedback on the value it may have to the receiver, not on the value of "release" that it provides the person giving the feedback.

9.  Focus feedback on the amount of information that the other person can use, not on the amount of information you have that you might like to give.

10.  Focus feedback on time and place so that personal issues can be shared at appropriate times.

11.  Focus feedback on WHAT is said rather than WHY it is said.

*Rate yourself (1, I do this well - to - 10, I need to improve in this area) on your effectiveness as a communicator and listener:*

_____ 1. Am I able to hear what is being said and implied about the person's attitudes and feelings without prejudging?

_____ 2. Am I able to listen and try to understand the thinking, motivation, and biases of the person in describing their situation and in working out any problems?

_____ 3. Do I try to put myself in their place and see the situation from their point of view?

_____ 4. Do I understand that not only have I the ability to influence others but they also have the ability to influence me?

_____ 5. Do I know my prejudices and my cultural assumptions and values so that they do not block out certain messages?

_____ 6. Do I understand that when a person feels they're is being understood, they tend to be more open?

_____ 7. Do I understand that people send messages in nonverbal ways and that I must "hear" this sort of communication, too?

_____ 8. Do I understand that being a good listener does not mean I must agree with what the speaker is saying?

_____ 9. Do I understand that I'm learning little when I am talking?

_____ 10. Do I try not to overreact to emotionally charged words?

_____ 11. When I disagree with something, do I make a special attempt to listen carefully?

_____ 12. If I am having trouble being understood, do I understand that the burden is on me to try to understand the other person?

_____ 13. Do I consider the person involved, as well as the situation?

_____ 14. Do I listen for what is not being said?

_____ 15. Do I listen for feelings behind the words as well as the words?

_____ 16. Do I look as if I am listening?

_____ 17. Do I know when I may be intimidating my listener by my threatening behavior?

## Reflection

*Thinking about the activities we did today, the Communication Quiz, and the workbook sheets, reflect on your strengths and weaknesses as a communicator and listener.*

_____

_____

_____

_____

_____

_____

_____

_____

_____

_____

_____

_____

_____

_____

_____

_____

_____

*Don't find fault.  Find a remedy.*
~Henry Ford

## Goals:

- To understand and practice concepts of consensus
- To challenge tendency to make decisions by "majority rule"
- To promote discussion on "chaos theory" in group dynamics

## Class Necessities:

- Student Workbooks
- "Choose A Color" envelopes
- Paper and pen/pencil for each student

## Class Outline:

The first half of the class will focus on a structured activity with each group member receiving a specific role to play.

Commence the class with a brief discussion on "Consensus" as a concept versus "Majority Rule" as a concept. Encourage students to address issues about the positives and negatives of each. In particular, be certain to address the issue of quiet individuals, people in the minority view of a group (whether by gender, race, belief, ability, etc.) and how majority rule can affect these people. Also discuss possible roles of leaders in these types of situations.

Do not discuss too deeply now, simply make certain that the students understand the difference between consensus and majority rule.

## Class Activity #1

### Choose A Color
### Goal: To understand concepts of consensus, negotiation, conflict management, and compromise.

Prior to class, copy and tape the GENERAL INSTRUCTIONS on the outside of one large envelope (9" x 12" or similar). Insert into this envelope, three smaller envelopes (business size or similar) with Envelope #1 having the ENVELOPE #1 instructions taped to the outside and each of the roles copied and cut into individual slips, inside.

Envelopes #2 and #3 should be identified as such but the instructions should be placed inside the envelopes respectively.

Up to sixteen students may participate. Additional students should be placed outside the participating group and serve as Observers to what happens. If you have fewer than 16 students, remove OBSERVER slips first, then select the slips you believe most appropriate to remove for your group's experience (if necessary).

When the participants have been identified, ask them to move to the center of the room. The individuals who are not participants will be identified as "Observers". There are also individuals in the participants group who will be "Observers" (determined by the slips of paper they choose). Ideally, your entire group can participate. The entire group should sit in a circle of chairs and the large envelope should be placed in the middle of the group. The large envelope should have the "General Instructions" taped or written clearly on the outside of it.

Briefly explain that they must read the instructions carefully from each envelope. Once they begin, reinforce that they are NOT TO SHARE their role with anyone else in either one of the groups (Volunteers or Observers). The Observers will have the job of watching what happens in the Volunteer's group. Neither group may talk with each other; and only volunteers may speak at all (among themselves) during the process.

........................................................................................................

## GENERAL INSTRUCTIONS

Enclosed you will find three envelopes that contain directions for this activity. Open Envelope I at once. Adhere to the time lines and open Envelopes II and III as instructed.

### *ENVELOPE I*

Time allowed: 15 minutes. Task: The group is to choose a color for your flag. Before deciding as a group which color to choose, each member is to take one of the small slips of paper from this envelope and follow the individual instructions within it. **DO NOT LET ANYONE SEE YOUR INDIVIDUAL INSTRUCTIONS.**

### *ENVELOPE II*

Time allowed: 5 minutes.
Task: You are to choose a group chairperson.

### *ENVELOPE III*

Time allowed: 10 minutes.
Task: You are to discuss the first part of this group activity in a discussion led by the newly elected chairperson. Ask your group if they want to stay in role or out of role for the discussion. If they choose to get out of role, have everyone read their slip of paper to the group prior to beginning the discussion.

# Roles

## *(copy and cut for students)*

1. You believe that everyone has an opinion and should be given the opportunity to express it. Your job is to make sure that everyone gives some input throughout the decision process. You support BLUE.

2. You are the tension-reliever and like to keep things going and make sure that things don't get tense, therefore, you must continually introduce NEW COLOR options, such as ORANGE.

3. You have a tendency to want to ask a lot of questions even if they aren't related to what the group is doing. Sometimes you even bring up totally unrelated topics to keep things lively! You support RED.

4. You are willing to have any color except you are against RED. You easily share your opinion with others in an effort to be helpful and you ask a lot of questions.

5. You are a non-traditionalist and will not accept a color from the PRIMARY colors, therefore, you should introduce non-traditional colors (MAGENTA, NEON GREEN, BRIGHT BLUE, etc.). The only traditional color you support is GREEN.

6. You are a follower. You tend to agree with anyone. You prefer YELLOW, but will support any shade of GREEN if it is brought to the discussion. You are against RED.

7. You continually give your opinion. In fact, you talk all of the time! You are against BLUE.

8. You have no preference for color, however, you are very much a team player. Therefore, when it sounds as if a decision is made, you must try to wrap the conversation up. You are against GREEN.

9. You have no faith that anything can get done in a group. You also would rather do it yourself or rely on past experience (i.e. "it's always been done this way"), therefore, whenever any new information is presented you are the one to find fault.

10. You have the special knowledge that the group is going to be asked to select a chairperson later. You are to conduct yourself in such a manner that they will select you as chairperson.

11. You have the special knowledge that the group is going to be asked to select a chairperson later. You are to conduct yourself in such a manner that they will select you as a chairperson.

12. You cannot stand conflict in your group! When people seem to be butting heads, you always jump in to prevent it from going any further. You do not want the color BLACK and the only time you will really get involved in conflict is when someone suggests it as a flag color!

13. You can't take anything seriously and are always making a joke about the group's goal. You make so many jokes and laugh so much that people start to not take you seriously. You don't like any color in particular and agree with everyone's ideas!

14. You are an OBSERVER. You have the job of watching what happens with the rest of the group. You may not speak with the others in the group. If you are asked for your opinion, strategically decline giving one.

15. You are an OBSERVER. You have the job of watching what happens with the rest of the group. You may not speak with the others in the group. If you are asked for your opinion, strategically decline giving one.

16. You are an OBSERVER. You have the job of watching what happens with the rest of the group. You may not speak with the others in the group. If you are asked for your opinion, strategically decline giving one.

Once your students have completed their "tasks" offer to assist the leader with the discussion (if necessary). You may simply offer them prompting questions, either verbally or having written them down to hand to the chairperson to use.

## Debrief:

- What did you discover during this process?
- Was it easy or difficult to stay in your role?
- How many of you had roles which were natural for you? How did that feel?
- How many of you had roles which were unnatural for you? How did that feel?
- What negotiations did you notice taking place?
- How did getting to consensus differ from majority rule?
- What are the pros and cons of using majority rule? What are the pros and cons of using consensus? When would each be most appropriate?
- What happens when your group has individuals who will not compromise or negotiate? (There is usually at least one in every group!)
- When conflict arose in your group, how was it managed?
- What happens when conflict in a group gets out of hand and it becomes unmanageable?
- How did the group respond to the deadlines and time limits given?
- How does this relate to your "real world" experiences?

Following the debriefing, have the group move to an area where they can think to themselves for the next activity. Indicate that different than the first activity, for this one they will not be given a specific role to play and they must use their own perspective.

**(Take Break or Use for next class session)**

## Class Activity #2:

Have them pull out a piece of paper and pen/pencil. While they are doing this, describe a scene where they are stranded on an island and they will be there for awhile. For the next few minutes, they must list the names of five (5) people who they believe can help them develop a community on that island and help them survive for a long time. Encourage them to select well known people, mainly because this facilitates an easier way for others to connect to the people they have selected. Although they do not necessarily have to write down their reasons for having each person on the island, they MUST be able to explain their reasons for having that person.

Once each person has listed their five people privately, have each student share their five people. Have a student volunteer (or yourself) write every name on the board. Also have a person write a summary list on a separate sheet of paper (to keep track, in case you run out of time!). As each person gives the names, they must also share their reason behind the choice.

When all of the names are on the board, indicate that a natural disaster has now reduced the island community and the entire class is now on one island. As a group, they are now to narrow down the entire list to only five (5) people to have there, in addition to the group.

At this point, have one of the students step forward to guide this process. The student facilitator should stand at the board, and work with the group to develop a process for selecting the best five people. Indicate that they should strive toward consensus as they attempt to narrow down the list. Other than this, your role should be to keep them on task, encourage people to speak up (if necessary), or any assistance with maintaining order! Check in with the group as they are getting close, and ask whether the decisions are still sensitive to consensus.

At the completion of the selection, or at a time prior to the end of the class session (giving time to discuss), process this experience (both in comparison to and separate from the first activity).

## Debrief:

- How did this differ from the first activity? Was it easier or more difficult?
- How did you advocate for the people you wanted?
- What happened when you "lost" one of your people from the list?
- How legitimate to survival were people's reasons for having certain individuals on their island?
- Were these reasons as important when you needed to narrow your choices further?
- What would have happened if the risk had been higher - that is, survival really was at stake?
- What happened to consensus during this process?
- Did it feel like others listened to you? If no, what would have happened to your view if you were working in a group which was really trying to come to consensus?
- Other questions relevant to your group's experience.

## Reflection: 
Page 27 or 28 (Alternate) of workbook.

Getting a group to come to CONSENSUS can be very difficult. Write your thoughts on what you experienced when choosing a color for your group flag as well as agreeing upon who will be on your "survival" island.

_____

_____

_____

_____

_____

_____

_____

_____

_____

_____

_____

_____

_____

_____

_____

_____

_____

_____

_____

*We all live under the same sky but we don't all have the same horizon.*
~Konrad Adenaur

## Ethical Decision Making | Class Plan

### Goals:
- To discuss the importance of Ethics and Values in leadership
- To be exposed to Kohlberg's Theory of Moral development
- To have productive discussion on ethical dilemmas
- To examine their own ethical decision making

## Class Necessities:
- Student Workbooks
- Flip chart/Markers or Classroom Board /Chalk

## Class Outline:

Introduce topic of Ethical Decision Making with prompting questions and using the outline of their workbook note page (in Ethical Decisions). Brainstorming as a class, establish working definitions of following words (sample definitions provided):

**Value -**
something which is of worth to an individual (whether beliefs, material goods, standards, etc.) (have the students brainstorm examples)

**Moral -**
principles or standards with respect to right and wrong in behavior/conduct —
typically, standards of right and wrong of a very personal or cultural nature (e.g. particular religions organizations, upbringings, etc. (have the students brainstorm examples)

**Dilemma -**
any situation requiring a choice between unpleasant alternatives (have the students brainstorm examples)

**Ethics -**
the study of standards of behavior and moral judgment — typically, society's standards of right and wrong (have the students brainstorm examples)


Discuss the role of each of these in our society;
Discuss the role in leadership situations—how do they apply to people who are leaders or who want to be leaders?

## Lecturette:

Present Lawrence Kohlberg's Theory — brief background — he was a psychologist who also cared deeply about philosophy (the study of principles and beliefs which underlie behavior, thought and the nature of the universe) — observed children between ages 10 - 16 and how they solved a series of dilemmas. Wanted to see why the kids answered questions not just whether they said "yes" or "no"

(This theory may be difficult for them to grasp, so simplify as appropriate!)
Make sure they take notes on their sheets.

He developed 6 stages—->

*Level I*  Called "Preconventional Morality" because people at this level do not yet think of themselves as members of society

**Stage 1**  "Obedience and punishment orientation"— decisions are based on the belief that powerful authorities hand down the rules and we must follow them — strongly based on punishment proving disobedience.

**Stage 2**  "Individualism and Exchange" — decisions based on the belief that rules are handed down but there is not just one right view of what is ethical or moral. See punishment as something one naturally wants to avoid.

*Level II* Called "Conventional Morality" because it assumes that the attitude toward ethics and morals would be shared by the entire community

**Stage 3**  "Good Interpersonal Relationships" — decisions based on the belief that people should live up to the expectations of the family and community and behave in "good" ways

**Stage 4**  "Maintaining the Social Order" — decisions based on obeying laws, respecting authority, and performing one's duties so that the social order is maintained

*Level III*    Called "Postconventional Morality" because it goes beyond the issue of laws and social order to decisions which will be maintain social justice and a commitment to your community

**Stage 5**  "Social Contract and Individual Rights" — People at this level believe that ethics and morality are meant to exist to make a good society and believe that people enter into a "contract" and move freely toward working for the benefit of all and that ethics exist so that people can maintain individual rights because they will do what is best and least harmful to others.

**Stage 6** "Universal Principles" — this is a very high level of thinking about ethics and achieving justice and believes that justice is universal and applies to all people regardless of what they do good or bad. Examples of leaders who reached this stage would be Gandhi; Martin Luther King, Jr.—they practiced ethics through civil disobedience (practicing peace in light of violence and laws)

## Class Activity:

Have the students read and respond to each of the dilemmas in their own books. After about 20-25 minutes (approximately), bring them back together as group and into a circle in the middle of room so that they are encouraged to speak with one another, especially when there are differences of opinion. Process each dilemma as a group. Debrief as appropriate.

## Additional Concepts of Ethical Decisions in Leadership

One model sees ethics as a hierarchy (something on top to something on bottom) and from the "Clearly Illegal" (or "Mandatory Ethics") which is very obvious, to the "Annoying" which is very unclear because what is annoying to one is not annoying to others!

Karen Kitchener says that all five of the characteristics on her list must be present if you are truly making an ethical decision. After reading through her sheet, ask them how often they really consider all of the aspects when they make ethical decisions (especially the doing no harm aspect!)

## Reflection:    Page 34 or 35 of workbook

Value:


Morals:


Dilemma:


Ethics:


Lawrence Kohlberg's Theory of Moral Development:

## Story One:
### Heinz and the Drug

In Europe, a woman was near death from a special kind of cancer. There was one drug that doctors thought might save her. It was a form of radium that a druggist in the same town had recently discovered. The drug was expensive to make, and the druggist was charging ten times what the drug cost to make. He paid $200 for the radium and charged $2,000 for a small dose of the drug. The sick woman's husband, Heinz, went to everyone he knew to borrow the money, but he could only get together about $1,000, which is only half of what it cost. He told the druggist that his wife was dying, and asked him to sell it cheaper or let him pay later. But the druggist said, "No, I discovered the drug and I'm going to make money from it." So Heinz got desperate and began to think about breaking into the man's store to steal the drug for his wife.

Should Heinz steal the drug?              Yes              No              Don't Know

List below all of the issues that go into your decision as to whether Heinz should or should not steal the drug.

## Story Two:
### Escaped Prisoner

A man had been sentenced to prison for 10 years. After one year, however, he escaped from prison, moved to a new area of the country, and took on the name of Thompson. For eight years he worked hard, and gradually he saved enough money to buy his own business. He was fair to his customers, gave his employees top wages, and gave most of his own profits to charity. Then one day, Mrs. Vigil, an old neighbor, recognized him as the man who had escaped from prison eight years before, and whom the police had been looking for.

Should Mrs. Vigil report Mr. Thompson to              Yes              No              Don't Know
the police and have him sent back to prison?

List below all of the issues that go into your decision as to whether Mrs. Vigil should or should not report Mr. Thompson to the police.

## Story Three:
### *Doctor's Dilemma*

A lady was dying of AIDS which could not be cured and she only had about six months to live. She was in terrible pain, but she was so weak that a good dose of pain-killer like morphine would make her die sooner. She was delirious and almost crazy with pain, and in her calm periods, she would ask the doctor to give her enough morphine to kill her. She said she couldn't stand the pain and that she was going to die in a few months anyway.

Should the doctor give her an overdose          Yes          No          Don't Know
of morphine that would make her die?

List below all of the issues that go into your decision as to whether the doctor should or should not give her the morphine that would make her die.


## Story Four:
### Newspaper

Fred, a senior in high school, wanted to publish a copied newspaper for students so that he could express many of his opinions. He wanted to speak out against some of the school's rules, like the no smoking rule. When Fred started his newspaper, he asked his principal for permission. The principal said it would be all right as long as before every publication Fred would turn in all of his articles for the principal's approval. Fred agreed and turned in several of the articles for approval. The principal approved all of them and Fred published two issues of the paper in the next two weeks.

     The principal had not expected that Fred's newspaper would receive so much attention. Students were so excited about the paper that they began to organize protests against the no-smoking regulation and other school rules. Angry parents objected to Fred's opinions. They phoned the principal telling him that the newspaper was unpatriotic and should not be published. As a result of the rising excitement, the principal ordered Fred to stop publishing.

Should the principal stop the newspaper?          Yes          No          Don't Know

List below all of the issues that go into your decisions as to whether the principal should or should not stop the newspaper.


*All dilemmas adapted from the Defining Issues Test by James Rest, 1979.*

Ethics is deciding what is right (or what is more right) in a particular situation. It means determining what ought to be, and deciding what is consistent with one's personal or organizational value system.

As leaders, you have hundreds of decisions to make — and as ethical leaders, you should try to make them in such a way that they are in the best interests of individuals, organizations, and the greater values of society. There are many different models and theories which can help a leader make ethical decisions. This model has been developed by W. Charles Redding and it may be useful to you as you make decisions as a leader.

Redding proposed that we think about all the decisions which we have to make, and organize them according to a hierarchy of their "badness" — from "most bad" to "least bad." The model is arranged in descending order of "badness."

• The Clearly Illegal (Mandatory Ethics)

• The Clearly Immoral or Unethical

• The Psychopathic: The Insane and therefore, Dangerous

• The Incredibly Stupid

• The Insensitive to Human Needs and Feelings

• The Inefficient or Impractical

• The Irritating or Annoying

When facing decisions, we first have to identify where the situation falls. In addition, we must figure out where (in the hierarchy) our tolerance level is — which situations will be tolerated, which are intolerable — and therefore, those with which we must deal.

*Adapted from information presented by Sara A. Boatman, Ph.D.*

"...ethical principles are more than convenient guidelines but less than absolutes. They are always ethically relevant, and they can be overturned only by stronger ethical obligations."

Kitchener believes that when making ethical decisions the following five areas should be considered in your decision.

## RESPECTING AUTONOMY

This is having freedom of thought or choice; allowing yourself and others to act as a "free agent"; showing respect for the rights of others.

## DOING NO HARM (non-maleficence)

This is avoiding inflicting physical and/or psychological harm on others; avoiding engaging in harmful or hurtful behavior, even unintentionally; being empathetic; trying to imagine how other feel.

## BENEFITING OTHERS (beneficence)

This is being kind and actively contributing to the general welfare of others; putting the welfare of others above your own interests.

## BEING JUST

This is being fair and impartial; treating others equally; considering the needs of undeserved populations that may need special attention or treatment.

## BEING FAITHFUL (loyalty)

This is recognizing implicit (or implied) contracts or agreements; entering into agreements in good faith; keeping promises, being loyal and telling the truth.

*Think about an "ethical dilemma" in your own life, either one with which you are currently struggling or one with which you dealt in the past. Write about how you are dealing (or dealt) with the dilemma using Kohlberg's or Kitchener's requirements for ethical decisions.*

_____

_____

_____

_____

_____

_____

_____

_____

_____

_____

_____

_____

_____

_____

_____

_____

*It is a random universe to which we bring meaning.*
~Henri Melamiel

## Goals:

- To introduce the concepts of teams and team building as they relate to leadership
- To highlight and promote how the class has moved (or can move) from being a "group" to becoming a "team"
- To develop a greater understanding of the role each student tends to naturally play when they are on a team
- To discuss the more "technical" aspects necessary or evident in a well-functioning team

## Class Necessities:

- Student workbook
- Open classroom or area (push all desks/tables & chairs to side of room)
- 16 or more balls/round items of various sizes and textures (rubber and plastic balls; small stuffed animals, bean bags; foam balls are not as useful unless they have some weight to them; do not use tennis balls or anything harder! All balls/items should be the size of softballs and smaller) *I find it useful to collect balls and "stuff" as I see them, and keep them in a 5 gallon paint tub.*
- Digital stopwatch or wristwatch with start/stop
- 11" x 17" sheets of paper (number in class plus one) ("Island Hopping")
- [If you opt for "Waste Management" activity, you will need: at least four (4) lengths of bicycle inner tube, cut into 12" - 16" lengths; 2 five (5) gallon tubs; several lengths (at least 4) of webbing, ranging from 6 feet to 15 or 20 feet; 15 foot rope, 35-50 foot rope (climbing ropes or other sturdy rope)] — This initiative alone, with set-up and debriefing can take 45 to 50 minutes. It may be useful at some other time if your class setting time is limited.

## Class Outline:

This class consists of a combination of team building activities designed to move the group toward becoming a more identifiable (to them) team. It consists of developing a higher level of trust and group involvement. This is only one group of activities, you may have others which would accomplish the same result. This sequence moves from:

- Warm-up & Shifting from "Group" to "Team" (Group Juggle/Warp Speed)
- Trust Sequence:     Trust Leans/Basics of trust techniques
                      Trust Triads
                      Yurt Circle
- Trust Falls
- Team Initiative/Problem Solving Activity (Island Hopping or Waste Management)

## Description of Activities:

## Group Juggle/Warp Speed

This is the same activity used during the Communication/Listening class session. This is deliberate, with the goal of using it being two-fold: (1) to allow the group to recognize the improvement of their skill at doing this activity; (2) to relate this improvement to them connecting as a "team" rather than simply a "group" of students in a class. Different than during the communication class, the set-up and debriefing of this activity should consist of "team" related concepts. As stated earlier in the guide, there are various ways of doing this activity. I prefer to begin the activity with one ball circling the group and ending the activity with a number of balls equal to the number of people in the group.

Have the students form a circle, all standing up, and no chairs in the way or being used. Ask them to brainstorm what characteristics are necessary for a team to be successful. Ask them also to reflect on how they see a "team" as different than a "group." (You may select to conduct other brief set-up comments to connect the students to the concept of team building.)

Let the group know that they are going to do the same ball activity from earlier, and this time they are to focus on the communication aspects as well as how each of them plays a role in their team. Remind them that they are a "friendly" group, and with that it means that they openly communicate with each other by stating one another's name when tossing the ball to each other. Describe their first goal being to set up a group pattern to get one ball around the circle. Remind them of the few rules that apply:

- The ball must be tossed to someone who is not directly next to the person tossing;
- Each person must catch and throw the ball only once;
- The last person to catch the ball cannot be the first person tossing the ball;
- The ball must remain in the air (i.e. bouncing it once is not appropriate);
- People should state the person's name prior to tossing (!);
- People should be aware of where they are tossing the ball (safety factor).

Once the group has established their ball pattern, indicate that you are now going to time them with that one ball. Time them the first time. The second time, ask them to set a group goal of the time it will take to get the ball around. Once they have completed the task with one ball, indicate that you believe they are capable of adding more balls, up to the number of people in the group. You will notice that they will be far less hesitant than the first time they did this activity. It is worth noting their response in order to incorporate it into the debriefing! Begin this phase of the activity by having them state how many balls they want to add to the "juggling" pattern. Again, they are to keep the same pattern, just adding more balls. Each time they establish the number of balls, have them successfully complete the pattern once, and then time them at least once. Continue this process until they end on a successful note and have added a significant number of balls.

## Debrief:

- Have the group discuss their successes and failures with this activity.
- How was this experience different than when you all did this earlier in the class?
- Did it feel different than before if you dropped the ball and stopped the pattern?  How did the group feel?
- What was important in terms of communicating with each other?
- How long did it take for everyone in the group to realize their part/role?
- What happened if someone had difficulty catching (or tossing) consistently? How did the group help?
- What impact did timing your pattern have on the group? On individuals?
- How do you think you did this activity different than before?  The same?
- How does this highlight your ability to work as a team?
- How can you apply this activity to real life and leadership?
- Other questions relevant to your group's experience.

Transition into the next activities by indicating that an important aspect of building a team is to trust each other.  (This typically comes out in their earlier brainstorm prior to the activities, so it may simply be that you reconnect them to the brainstorm by remarking: "An earlier comment you made was that trust was important.  Our next activities are going to focus on this!)

## Trust Sequence:

People conduct trust activities in various ways.  The consistent factors are that trust requires SAFETY and paying attention.  Therefore, regardless of which trust activities you use, make certain that all participants are paying attention as you describe any guidelines or expectations!

### Trust Leans:

These are the most fundamental aspects of developing trust.  Have the students partner up with someone with whom they are comfortable and/or would like to work with in developing trust.  Have a student volunteer to be your partner for the demonstration stage of the activity.  Use this student to be either the catcher or leaner as you explain the logistics of the activity (below).

Trust leans are designed to assist participants with getting a sense of relying on another person for a low-risk and controllable situation.  Each partner has a role to play:

*Catcher/Support Person:* This person is the one who will be "catching" the other person as they lean back onto their hands. They are to take a position (standing) behind the leaner, putting their strongest foot forward, holding their arms up to the leaner's back (about shoulder blades), with hands slightly cupped (fingers not stiff, but rather slightly cupped to support the weight of the other person). At the point of the person leaning, they will reasons to "commands" issued by the leaner.

*Leaner/Faller:* This person is the one who will be "falling" or "leaning" into the hands of the other person. They should stand with their back to their catcher, feet shoulder width apart, butt tucking in (I sometimes draw the analogy of having to hold a coin in their butt and holding it as to prevent it from falling!). Their arms should be folded up against their chest (elbows in; hands clasped). The leaner will begin the commands to make certain the catcher is ready PRIOR to falling. When the leaner leans, s/he should roll slightly on their heels, being certain to keep their body stiff. Falling any other way, such as bending at the hip, or stepping back, is a clear indicator that they didn't quite trust the other person. Have them practice.

The commands exchanged are:

(Leaner):     "Catcher Ready"
(Catcher):    "Ready"
(Leaner):     "Falling"
(Catcher):    "Fall Away"

At the point of "Fall Away," the leaner should roll back. Have each group practice several times, with both partners experiencing both catching and leaning. They can increase their trust with one another by having the leaner close her/his eyes prior to falling, asking the catcher to catch the leaner closer to the ground, etc. Make sure that you emphasize the importance of the commands and the necessity to be paying attention to one another.

Once the students have experienced both leaning and catching, they may choose to do this same activity but with three people. In this case, there is one person in the middle who is caught by a person both in front of them and behind them. The commands are the same. The person in front should catch the person about halfway down the arms (folded in front), between the shoulder and the elbow. The person leaning must be certain to tell his/her catchers which way s/he is falling first! They may increase risk/trust by closing their eyes or asking their catchers to allow them to lean further each time. Again, emphasize safety!

## Yurt Circle:

Transition the group from the fundamental trust activity to "Yurt Circle" by asking the entire group to gather into a circle. They should hold hands, without interlocking fingers. Indicate that they are now to trust the entire group and work with the entire group to support one another. Have the group count off by twos (1,2,1,2,1,2...), making certain that the group count ends with a 1 next to a 2, not two of the same numbers as neighbors. If this happens because of your group size, you should step in to provide the balance necessary. (Students love this too, because it demonstrates in a very subtle way your level of trust for/with them).

State that on the count of three, the Ones will all roll gently forward, as they did in the trust leans; and the Twos will roll gently back. They are to be conscientious that they are not putting all of their weight unnecessarily into the lean. Rather, their goal as a group is to have a nicely balanced circle. Indicate that you will also count to three for them to roll back to the center.

This is an easy and powerful activity for the group because of the need for balancing each other and how much they realize that they are capable of holding up others, regardless of weight/height.

## Trust Falls:

This activity is a higher progression of the trust sequence. In this case, the person who is falling will do so from a sturdy table and/or desk which is at least three feet off the ground. Your resources may vary, however to do this activity the falling spot needs to have clearance above the faller and the faller must have their knees at least six inches above where the catchers support system will meet them (to prevent causing the knees to "buckle" when falling.)

The first faller should climb onto the designated platform. The rest of the class should create two parallel lines, facing each other, from the platform. The two lines will create a safe landing spot by putting their arms at a ninety degree angle in front of them (bending the arms, palms up, at the elbow toward the other line). Their arms should alternate with the person across from them, forming a "zipper" effect. The palms must be flat, no fists! The catchers should stand with their feet shoulder width apart and shoulder to shoulder with the person next to them. IN order for this to be safe, the lines must consist of at least five people minimum (ten total). They can easily consist of more, or if your group is very large, have the others spot as well.

The faller's stance is the same as when s/he practiced with a partner. The commands prior to falling are the same. When the faller calls "Catcher's Ready" and they respond, "Ready", it should mean that they are "zippered up" and looking at the back of the faller. In addition, make certain the group recognizes that they need to be prepared to put the person down on the ground once they have fallen (preferably feet first!).

Often, I will have a student lie on the ground underneath the zippered up hands (between the lines) so that they can watch the person fall. They get a kick out of this! Your command prior to the group falling should be "Zipper Up," at which point the group should get into their prepared safety mode, ready for their faller to state her/his commands.

*Important Set Up information:*
Spend a few minutes discussing with the group the "physics" of the body and how weight is distributed. Make certain that they are aware of the heaviest spots and that they pay

attention to keeping the head safe. This is a very safe activity when done correctly and conscientiously. You may choose to refrain from this activity for groups who are too hyper or who can't even take the trust leans/fundamentals seriously!

## Debrief :

- How did the group feel prior to the activities and after?
- What was learned by participating in these activities?
- How do the characteristics of the activities relate to building a team?
- What role did each person play?
- How has their level of trust for others in the group changed?
- What happens in building a team if people are not sensitive to the strengths and weaknesses of each member?
- What characteristics did you observe in all of the activities that relate to team building?
- As a leader, how do you develop a team when people do not trust one another?
- Any other questions relevant to your group experience.

The next two activities are group initiatives. They take 30 to 45 minutes each, therefore you should select one to use for this class session. You may have others which you would prefer to use. The goal, regardless of what activity you use, is to move the group to an even higher level of working together as a team. The activity chosen should also fit into the progression or sequence developed in this class session. The selection and fit of the activities allows debriefing to connect all of the activities and the related experiences of the group/group members.

## Island Hopping:

In the center of the room, lay the pieces of 11" x 17" paper in a line, with 6 to 8 inches in between each sheet. You should lay down the number of sheets of paper, PLUS one, as there are students in the class. These are to become your islands. Split the group into two, and have each student step onto an island, leaving the very center island empty. Each side should have an equal number of students, and each "side" should be facing the center. The goal of the initiative is to get the two groups of people to exchange places on the line.

Often, I will create a scene where the islands are floating in rough water (or radioactive water, or sewage, etc. —- be creative!) and if you step off you loose the use of your foot, arm, etc. (depending upon how many times a person steps off!). There are several "rules" to explain:

YOU MAY:
- You must move into an empty place
- Only move around a person who is facing you
- Have only one person move at a time

YOU MAY NOT:
- Move backwards
- Move around someone who is facing the same way you are
- Move at the same time as any other person

There are various ways to accomplish this initiative. In general, the most efficient groups usually discover that this initiative is best solved if one person is allowed to "lead" the others through it.

## Debrief:

- How did the group ultimately solve this problem?
- What was it like when you had an idea and no one listened?
- What was it like when others were moving and you were still "stuck" on your island?
- How can a team be sensitive that not everyone has the same perspective on things?
- What characteristics were important to keep your group together?
- (If one person took over) How did the team feel when you began to rely upon (name)?
- What did you think about their style of communicating to the rest of the team?
- For those of you who became "followers," how did it feel to have that role?
- Now that you've accomplished this, what would you have changed early in the process?
- How does this activity relate to leadership?
- What did you learn from working with the rest of your team?
- Other questions relevant to your group's experience.

## Waste Management:

The object of this initiative is to have the team transfer all of the balls that are in one container to another, using only the "resources" provided.

*Set up -*
The smaller rope should be placed in the center of the room, in a circle approximately 3 to 4 feet in diameter. Inside this circle, you should place the two 5 gallon tubs, one full of balls, stuffed animals, and other items; and the other empty (open side up).

The larger rope should be placed in a circle surrounding the smaller circle, with at least 5 or 6 feet between the diameter of the two. The resources should be placed beside the outside circle, in no particular order.

*Rules:*

The object is to transfer all of the items from one container to the other, using the resources provided. The transfer must take place within the smaller circle. Any knots can be tied in the webbing or rubber pieces. All of the resources are to be used "as is", meaning no cuts can be made on any of them. No one may enter or make contact with the area between the two ropes nor onto the "island" in the middle. If ground contact is made, the person who touches must sit out for thirty seconds, including being silent.

After explaining the rules to the group, indicate that they have 35 minutes total to complete the task. This includes discussing and planning, as well as executing their plan. If the group needs additional time to complete the task, have them negotiate for time in increments, but in any case, let them complete the task.

## Debrief:

- How did the group accomplish this task?
- How well did people work together?
- How well did people communicate?
- What were the frustrations of this task? How did your group attempt to resolve them?
- How well did the group strategize? How well did you recover when mistakes were made?
- What did you learn from your mistakes?
- For those of you who did not participate a lot, why didn't you? (usually they feel like their voice wasn't heard by others in the group?)
- Did anyone have an idea that the group did not listen to or that you did not share? Why?
- What were the strengths of your team in this activity? Weaknesses?
- How did people share responsibility in the group?
- Other questions relevant to your group's experience.

## Closure of Class:

Regardless of the activities used, bring the class together to synthesize the experiences and the application of the team building concepts. Read through, as a group, the sheets on team building, and discuss/apply appropriately.

## Reflection:    Page 40 or 41 (Alternate) of workbook.

*"Human beings possess the unique capability of working together to produce a result that is greater than the sum of the individual talents which enter into the task." ~ John Paul, 1980*

*"Teamwork is the ability to work together toward a common vision. The ability to direct individual accomplishment toward organizational objectives. It is the fuel that allows common people to attain uncommon results!"*

- A team is a group of people who work together to achieve a desired outcome.
- People become a true team when they work together to accomplish something.
- Teamwork is the behaviors in a group that complement and support each other.
- Teamwork is required in any situation in which more than one person is needed to accomplish a task.
- Teamwork is important for any team that participates in deciding who will do what & how goals will be achieved.

We can increase the possibilities for productive output for a group through the use of team building. Team building is a two-step process by which "groups" become "teams" by first focusing on barriers to effective group work & process, and the to enact changes to remove those barriers and improve group effectiveness.

*Team building allows the following:*
- Members are given the chance to examine the way they interact & relate to one another.
- Members can observe the group process in both how they work together as a team, and how they work as individuals within the team.
- Members can observe the way decisions are made and implemented.
- Members can increase the confidence and trust that they have for one another.
- Team builders can help members realize the amounts of power and influence individual members hold, and the ways the power is used.

Team builders can make group members feel more comfortable with one another, make individuals feel as though they are a part of the group, help members gain trust for one another, and teach members how to work together as a "team."

Groups may not openly express feelings. Team builders create communication and build a cohesive, supportive, trusting group where members feel free to express feelings and ideas. As members develop the trust and feeling of belonging to the group, they make a commitment to the group and take responsibility in group participation. As group members get involved, things begin to happen and the group begins to accomplish and produce greater than the sum of the individual talents in the group.

*To build an effective team, you must:*
- Know the skills, abilities, needs, and fears of your members.
- Provide an atmosphere to foster open, honest communication.
- Build a positive social relationship with members.
- Communicate frequently through visits, meetings, etc.
- Delegate responsibility to members.
- Trust each other to complete assigned tasks.
- Provide mutual support.
- Build respect for each other to complete assigned tasks.
- Use the uniqueness or special skills of each member to accomplish your goals.
- Build pride for your group.

A TEAM CAN EXIST ONLY WHEN ALL PLAYERS UNDERSTAND THAT THEY SHARE A COMMON FATE! EVERYONE MUST BE COMMITTED TO WORKING TOGETHER. A SENSE OF "TEAMWORK" EXISTS:

- When the project is equally important to all team members;
- When each person clearly understands his or her role in the process & the roles of the other members of the team;
- When each team member accepts every other team member as an important contributor to the task at hand;
- When each person values the contributions of others equally;
- When all contributions are acknowledged;
- When integrity and trust are established through open communication and honesty;
- When the team members realize that good teamwork is a process. It cannot be accomplished overnight!

*Requirements for teamwork:*
- Common/shared goals and the desire to achieve them
- Knowledgeable, skilled team members
- Trust in one another
- Respect for one another
- Willingness to take risks
- A winning attitude and good leadership
- Dedication
- A system for supporting one another
- A well-organized structure
- Synergy — the belief that the team is more than the sum of its parts
- Feeling like you belong
- Honesty
- Participation and good relationships among team members

*Leaders often do not think team building is important because they have not considered the advantages that can come from a strong team effort. Following are some results of team performance.*

- Realistic, achievable goals can be established for the team and individual members because those responsible for doing the work contribute to their construction.

- Leaders and team members commit to support each other to make the team successful.

- Team members understand one another's priorities & help or support when difficulties arise.

- Communication is open. The expression of new ideas, improved work methods, and talking about problems and concerns is encouraged.

- Problem solving is more effective because the expertise of the team is available.

- Performance feedback is more meaningful because team members understand what is expected and can monitor their performance against expectations.

- Conflict is understood as normal and viewed as an opportunity to solve problems. Through open discussion it can be resolved before it becomes destructive.

- Balance is maintained between group productivity & the satisfaction of individual member's needs.

- The team is recognized for outstanding results, as are individuals for their personal contributions.

- Members are encouraged to test their abilities and try out ideas. This becomes infectious and stimulates individuals to become stronger performers.

- Team members recognize the importance of disciplined work habits and conform their behavior to meet standards.

- Learning to work effectively as a team in one group, is good preparation for working as a team with other groups.

- Teamwork and productivity go hand in hand!

## A WELL-FUNCTIONING TEAM:

1   The team shares a sense of purpose or common goals and each team member is willing to work toward achieving these goals.

2.  The team is aware of, and interested in its own processes and norms in the group.

3.  The team identifies its own resources and uses them, depending on the team's needs at any given time.  The team also lets different people lead, depending on their strengths.

4.  Group members continually try to listen to and clarify what is being said and are interested in what others say and feel.

5.  Differences of opinion are encouraged and freely expressed.

6.  The team is willing to bring forward conflict and focus on it until it either is resolved or managed in a way  that does not reduce the effectiveness of the individuals involved.

7.  The team gives energy toward problem solving rather than allowing it to be drained by interpersonal issues  or competitive struggles.

8.  Roles are balanced and shared, allowing for the accomplishment of task and feelings of the group sticking together and maintaining high morale.

9.  To encourage risk taking and creativity, mistakes are treated as sources of learning rather than reasons for punishment.

10. The team is responsive to the changing needs of its members and to the external environment which surrounds it.

11. Team members support each other to regularly evaluate the team's performance.

12. The team is attractive to its members, who identify with it and consider it a source of both professional and personal growth.

13. Developing a climate of trust is recognized as the crucial element for supporting all of the above elements for the team.

*Think about today's team and/or a team on which you are a member. What makes that team an effective team or an ineffective team? Why do you enjoy or dislike being a member of the team? What would you change to make your team more effective?*

_____

_____

_____

_____

_____

_____

_____

_____

_____

_____

_____

_____

_____

_____

_____

_____

_____

_____

_____

*I am because we are.*
~Eric Utne

## Goals:

- To introduce students to concepts related to gender, leadership, and communication styles
- To discuss and experiment with stereotyped beliefs about how men and women lead
- To investigate and apply various gender-related concepts
- To challenge student perspectives of men and women in their beliefs and actions.

## Class Necessities:

- Student Workbook
- Flip chart
- Markers

## Class Outline:

This can be a difficult class topic, depending upon the maturity of your group. You may choose not to do this topic, or to conduct it in a manner different than described, depending upon the needs of your group. In addition, if you have a single-gender group, you will need to modify appropriately. In those cases, single gender groups lend themselves to good discussions, rather than the activity described. The activity can still be conducted, simply with groups not separated by gender, and the following discussion can still be very informative.

Introduce the class to the topic of gender differences by writing the terms GENDER and SEX on the board. Have the class define the differences of the two and give examples for each.

GENDER should be defined as the norms, stereotypes, expectations based on social or cultural values. These generally do not describe every person of alike, for example, one gender stereotype is that "men don't cry" or that "women should not work". Discuss examples with the class, as well as ways that gender expectations are expressed by generation or other characteristic.

SEX should be defined as the biological differences — that is you are born MALE or FEMALE. Your GENDER (or identity) is obviously tied to your SEX, but the two are different descriptors, and one does not exclude the other. Discuss the terms MASCULINE and FEMININE as well. Include discussion on how these terms also relate to stereotypes or generalizations and that not all individuals of one sex (OR gender) fit the descriptors.

After this interchange, move onto the class activity. Indicate that the class is going to "test" some theories about gender differences and that they will also get the chance to see that sex and gender sometimes go hand in hand, but often, how gender is expressed is very personal and individual, and may not fit the stereotype of their sex.

## Class Activity:

Separate your class into two groups, one of all boys and one of all girls. Give each group markers and flip chart paper to use for their "group project". Have each group create their perfect organization. Write the following list on the board or on a flip chart to place in front of the room so that the groups can refer to it as they are creating their organization. On sheets of paper, the groups should include descriptions/explanations for the following:

• Organization Name
• Organization Mission/Goals
• What issues are important for your organization?
• What positions exist in your organization?
• What is the atmosphere of your organization?
• What benefits does your organization have (health, retirement, day-care, family leave, )
• What styles of leadership exist?
• How are decisions made?
• What are the ethics/values of your organization?
• What are the roles of each person in your group?
• How do you resolve conflict?
• How do you deal with power?
• How do you solve problems?
• How do you deal with change or crisis?
• How is money dealt with in your organization?
• How do people move up in your organization?
• Do your leaders get involved on projects?
• How do you evaluate achievements?

Once the groups have completed their "projects", have each designate a spokesperson. The spokesperson should explain the organization and their responses to each question. Allow others to ask clarifying questions. You may comment on your observations before you have discuss as a class, or offer your observations after the class discusses.

## Debrief:

• What similarities did the group's see? What differences?

• Ask each group, how did you get the end result you have?

• How did each group work together?

- What would you have changed about how your group worked together?

- Was there anyone in your group who did not like how your group completed the project?

- Did you speak up?

- What happened when you didn't agree with things decided upon by the group?

- What things in this process do you think occurred because of gender? What about sex?

- Do you think that two other groups of all men or all women would have the same outcome?

- What do you think would be different if your groups were both co-ed?

- Other questions relevant to your group's experience.

After the debriefing and observations, finish the student workbook page which highlights the differences of styles (Gilligan's research). Then go through the page highlighting the differences between MODERN (or feminine) and TRADITIONAL (or masculine) leadership styles. This page can be challenging because some students start to see traditional as "bad" ways of leading, rather than recognizing the differences and the necessities of both styles. Discuss as appropriate and necessary.

| **Reflection:** | Page 44 or 45 (Alternate) of workbook. |

Men & women have different styles in communicating and leading. Some of the differences are based on stereotypes and social expectations; some of the differences are based on true gender differences. The important thing to remember is that both men & women can have MASCULINE AND FEMININE traits in leading and communication. In the past, the masculine leadership is what ran businesses and countries. As time has gone on, feminine traits have become a natural part of leadership styles.

We will refer to these different styles as "Traditional" and "Modern." Do not look at them as good or bad, simply different. In general, feminine leadership styles align more with the Modern approach and masculine leadership styles align more with Traditional approaches. Again, regardless of your sex (being male or female) you may approach situations with a combination of Traditional and Modern styles.

Write down what you think are the differences between "Gender" and "Sex:"

Gender                                    versus                                    Sex

Just like Lawrence Kohlberg (see Ethical Decision Making section of workbook) researched moral development, Carol Gilligan also did research on moral development. She looked at differences between men and women as they approached working with others to solve moral problems and leadership. She found the following "differences" between men and women:

## *Women and things that are important in leading others:*
Caring for others; Being sensitive and responsible to others; Connecting with others; Measuring quality by the relationships they have with others; Sharing Power; Making decisions in the situation being dealt with; empowering others; and building upon similarities with others

## *Men and things that are important in leading others:*
Fairness & Justice; Individual rights; Independence and separation from others; Measuring qualities by personal success and achievement; Hierarchical power (top to bottom); Making decisions based on rules and logic; self-empowerment; and on being different from others.

Gender-related leadership and communication styles are GENERALIZATIONS. This means that not all men and not all women are alike. Both genders may have characteristics of the other gender when they lead. Actual leadership behaviors depend upon culture, values, upbringing, role of gender in a person's life, family and social expectations, among other things. Most men and women practice leadership which is a mix of both MODERN and TRADITIONAL styles!

*Mariam MacGregor, Copyright © 2000*

## Traditional Leadership Model ("Masculine")

| | |
|---|---|
| How Things Get Done: | Competition |
| Organizational Structure: | Hierarchy |
| Expectations: | Winning |
| How Problems are Solved: | Rational |

### Key Characteristics
High control, strategic, unemotional, analytical

### Power
Among Traditional leaders, "position" power tops the list of frequently used styles.

### Outcomes
While the Traditional approach tends to be faster, it does not encourage working with others, shared accountability or participation in problem-solving. The Traditional approach relies more heavily on things outside the organization.

### Teamwork
The lessons through traditional activities often have less to do with teamwork than they do with competitiveness and winning. Traditional team sports do not teach the same positive human values as cooperative games do.

### Participation
Many Traditional leaders see increased member participation in decision-making as a breakdown of their influence and in some cases, a threat to stability of the organization.

### Relationships with Others
Many Traditional leaders regard relationships as a means to an end ("making connections") rather than regarding the relationship as important alone.

### Conflict Management
Traditional leaders prefer a competitive response to conflict, frequently seen as a "win-lose" approach. The other type of behavior favored is "avoidance".

### Problem Solving
Many Traditional leaders still over-rely on measurable ways to identify solutions to complex problems. Collecting data and information is how they effectively problem solve.

### Pitching In
Many Traditional leaders believe that pitching in with the group can tarnish their image as the leader.

## Modern Leadership Model ("Feminine")

| | |
|---|---|
| How Things Get Done: | Cooperative |
| Organizational Structure: | Team |
| Expectations: | Quality Output |
| How Problems are Solved: | Intuitive/Rational |

### Key Characteristics
Lower control, empathetic, collaborative, high standards

### Power
Modern leaders tend to use "personal" power to influence the organization and motivate others.

### Outcomes
The Modern approach often helps create a more cooperative atmosphere by encouraging participation and shared accountability. The Modern approach draws more on the internal resources.

### Teamwork
Connectedness and building networks where one is at the center rather than hierarchies, where someone is on top, are elements of Modern leadership.

### Participation
Participation by all members is the philosophy for Modern leaders, including high communication, member input, encouraged creativity, and increased autonomy.

### Relationships with Others
For Modern leaders, establishing & maintaining effective relationships is a cornerstone on which this approach is built.

### Conflict Management
Modern leaders work together with others to resolve conflict, and seek to find different, more satisfying solutions to complex problems than those proposed by either side. The other type of behavior favored is "accommodation" (finding room for everyone).

### Problem Solving
Inductive reasoning (trusting a feeling) is used and allows the leader to solve problems with less measurable information. It is often more innovation-directed and is valued in organizations because it has to do with working with people.

### Pitching In
Most Modern leaders are willing to put themselves into any situation and helping out.

*Adapted from work by A.W. Schaef (1981)*

*Think about the activity we did today, the differences in styles that we explored, and about how you relate to others in general. Write about which characteristics of the different styles (Modern or Traditional) describe your own style.*

---
---
---
---
---
---
---
---
---
---
---
---
---
---
---
---
---
---
---

*The history of every country begins in the heart of a man or woman.*
~Willa Cather

## Goals:
- To introduce students to the concepts of tolerance and diversity within leadership
- To challenge students to examine their own prejudices & the impact these beliefs may have in their roles as leaders
- To encourage productive dialogue on social values regarding diversity and managing conflict in diverse groups

## Class Necessities:
- Student Workbook
- PBS Video - (from Frontline Series) — A Class Divided (Video is 1 hour exactly)

This video is generally available at Public Libraries or through PBS Video Collection Catalogue. In addition, check with your district's Media Center or at a local college or Public library.
- For second class session on this topic, "Awareness Stretch" & Lecturette
- Also for second class, flip chart paper/markers

***For video purchase, contact:***
PBS Video Collection 1320 Braddock Place Alexandria, VA 22314  1.800.344.3337
Cost: $200.00 (includes copy of the accompanying book by same name)

## Class Outline:

### Introduce Diversity and Tolerance Concepts

Prompting questions to focus topic—

- Why is tolerance of people's differences important in leadership roles?
- How does the behavior of a leader affect an organization in terms of acceptance and tolerance of people's differences?
- What is the impact to your organization if you (as a leader) are not aware of your prejudices & biases?
- Other questions which relate directly to your school's culture.

### Define Terms:

Introduce each term and have students brainstorm definitions and gather examples of the behavior or belief.  Have the students take notes in their workbooks on the definitions the class agrees to. (Sample definitions follow).

**Diversity:**

Recognizing differences, variety, and possessing various characteristics. Diversity is seen as pleasurably distracting the attention from something that is burdensome, oppressive, or otherwise limiting by incorporating different characteristics and beliefs.

**Tolerance:**

"Tolerance" can be defined in a variety of ways — in general, get them to the point of understanding that tolerance is the ability to respect others' beliefs and practices, etc. without necessarily sharing the same beliefs. With regards to diversity issues, Tolerance means more than "just putting up with" (which is also a definition of the term)

**Prejudice:**

An opinion held in disregard of facts that contradict it. A preconceived, usually unfavorable idea.

**Phobia:**

An irrational , excessive, and persistent fear of something or a situation.

**Bias:**

Partiality or preference for one thing over another. Bias is not necessarily a bad thing, it can mean that one prefers one interest (say, music) over another (hiking). It is when biases became the basis for decisions which are negative (say, leadership decisions) and affect one group to "lose out" to the wishes of others (such as, only certain people in the group can vote).

**-Ism:**

A suffix which makes theory out of the term in reference (e.g., racism, sexism, ageism, etc.).

## Preface Video:

Put into context that it is a late 70s/early 80s film and although things were perceived and addressed differently then, there is significant relevance to what is happening today.

Encourage them to pay attention to how easily children AND adults were persuaded to be biased and prejudiced without much encouragement!

(Jot down notes on any statements which stand out in the video to use during debriefing)

## Debrief:

• What affected you the most? (What "buttons" did the video push?)

• How does this video apply to anyone's roles as leaders?

- How aware are they of their prejudices and influence on others?
- When it comes to diversity issues, who has had the most influence on you (good or bad) in terms of how you treat others?
- What would happen if this same experiment was conducted today?
- If a leader continues being prejudiced or discriminates against people, what is the impact?
- Other questions relevant to your group?

## Leadership & Tolerance Class Session #2

This class session can be particularly challenging because it forces the students to evaluate their own perspectives of people who are different than themselves. It is important to continue the class standard of mutual respect, which by this time, should be well established among the students (and yourself!).

Briefly review video—Ask students if there is anything which they have reflected upon since previous session or any remaining thoughts on the video.

Introduce this class session as an opportunity to explore the various positions that people take when interacting with different populations. They will evaluate their own beliefs and will explore the various opinions and behaviors of class members relating to leadership and tolerance.

## Introduce Awareness Stretch:

*(Page for Notes in Student Handbook)*

The Awareness Stretch is one way to "test" ourselves on tolerance and understanding. Starting at Non-Aware, explain what each level means (have students take notes as appropriate); where there are examples, feel free to incorporate your own related to the populations with whom you are working:

*Non-Aware:*
This level describes someone who does not know that differences exist. An example would be someone who grew up in a rural area who visits a big city without knowing that distinct differences occur. Another example would younger children who are not aware that there are differences in their family traditions and activities until they begin attending school or stay over at a friend's house. We can generally refer to this stage as "Naive" (define) because the person does not know anything else than by what they are surrounded.

*Awareness:*
This level describes someone who realizes that there are differences between people, lifestyles, or populations because they have OBSERVED these differences. Using the above

example, a person who lives in a rural area visits a big city and sees the hustle and bustle or interactions among people. The child stays over at a friend's house and celebrates a cultural event with them. After becoming AWARE, people can "choose" to move up the Stretch by increasing their awareness of these differences or they can move down, to Denial.

## Denial:

Choosing to deny that differences exist can lead to ongoing "Ignorance" (ignoring the differences). This is where violence and discrimination occurs because the person continues behaviors which deny the contributions and characteristics of people different than themselves.

## Acceptance:

This level describes when a person moves another step through the stretch by reflecting on the differences and accepting that people have a right to be difference or "diverse."
Understanding: This level is reached by taking acceptance even further. A person at this level continues to find out more about the differences of people through: Reading and researching; communication with others (person-to-person); traveling to new places; discussions; attending cultural events and festivals; reflection within self; learning a new language; hosting others who are different than themselves, etc. The level of understanding requires risks to be taken because people find out a lot about themselves while they are finding out about others!

## Appreciation:

Reaching this level means that someone has spent time, energy, discovery, etc. at the understanding level and taken it to the "Nth" degree. These people develop new relationships with different people based on similarities. They celebrate the differences and continue to expose themselves and others to the diversity. People at this level also recognize that people come from different backgrounds and upbringing and that developing relationships with others is important to understand these differences. People at this level have become comfortable and consistent with their beliefs regarding diversity.

After presenting each level, prompt discussion regarding the stretch. This may take on various forms. An important portion of the discussion should touch on the fact that people may be at different places on the Stretch for different populations. This is a difficult concept for some to grasp, particularly if they are extremely dualistic and see diversity awareness as "all or nothing" concepts. Understanding that some people may not be in the appreciation level for everything, is also difficult for highly tolerant students to understand because they will expect all people to be at that level. In addition, spend time discussing that each level may be very difficult to move to and that many adults (and leaders!) are not very high on the stretch! (Perhaps have them provide examples).

## Simulation through the Stretch :

Break class into groups of three. Encourage the groups to be diversely comprised. If you have a racially/culturally homogenic group, encourage distribution by gender, age, leadership position, or some other diversity. Have each group select one of the groups identified on the "Reflection" (p. 49); make sure each student group has a different group.

Give each group a piece of flip chart paper and several markers. Have each small group write down and describe the behaviors that would be demonstrated at each level with regard to their "population". In addition, have them describe what a person would have to do to move up a level on the Stretch. Encourage specificity! For example, at the Understanding stage, rather than saying "read a book about the culture" or "attend a festival" encourage the students to state a particular book or specific culturally relevant event.

If there are students within the class who represent one of the cultures/beliefs, encourage the students to ask them (this is particularly powerful for discussion! Especially if students have assumed the background of a person). When having them ask questions of others, have them present it as : "Is there anyone here who is (blank) and who can help us with examples from their own lives?" Again, it is cautionary to remind students that not all people from the same culture have the same experience and the only way to explore the differences is to ASK!

Give students a minimum of 15 minutes to complete this group task (it may easily take longer). Once each group has completed, have them present their steps and examples through the stretch. Bring class back together for debrief.

## Debrief:

- Was this easy or difficult to do?
- What were your initial reactions when reflecting on your own beliefs about the population your group selected?
- How did you deal with conflict in your group, especially when someone could not visualize or understand how to move up a level?
- What similarities existed in your group about this population? What differences?
- How does the Stretch apply to INDIVIDUALS versus GROUPS? Are there differences? Similarities?
- How did it feel to ask your peers about specifics of their own culture? Were assumptions made about others prior to this activity?
- Did others make assumptions about you? How did that feel and how did you respond?
- What have you become aware of with regards to your own beliefs, behaviors, and tolerance?
- Do you need to change? Do you want to change?
- How does the Stretch relate to leadership? How about YOUR leadership skills?
- Other relevant questions to your class and their experiences?

## Reflection: Page 49 or 50 (Alternate) of workbook.

Leaders who do not understand their own prejudices can create an environment of distrust, blame, and negativity in their organizations and with their friends. In addition, many people look to leaders to do the right thing with regards to racial issues, gender relations, and in general, all social issues related to tolerance.

If, as a leader, you are racist or sexist or intolerant in any other ways, how do you think this will impact those who look to you for leadership?

## Definitions:

Diversity:

Tolerance:

Prejudice:

Phobia:

Bias:

-Ism:

The Awareness Stretch is a way to "test" your multicultural competence, that is, how aware you are of your own prejudices and/or areas of challenge. Each level of the stretch represents how we move through understanding people who are different than ourselves. It is called a stretch because when we are honest with ourselves, we may have to explore our personal outer limits with regards to different populations.

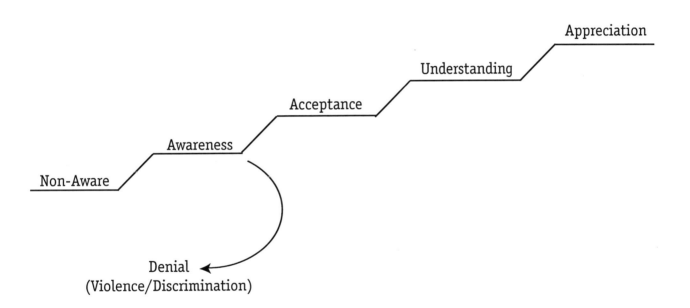

Non-Awareness:

Denial:

Awareness:

Acceptance:

Understanding:

Appreciation:

*Reflect on where you are on this scale with the following groups and how your feelings about people in these groups (and as individuals) can affect the type of leader you are (be honest with yourself) (this list is only to get you thinking, you can add any others with whom you interact or choose not to interact):*

African-American/Black • Asian-American/Pacific Islander • European-American/Anglo • Latino/a - Mexicano/a - Chicano/a • Native-American • Gay/Lesbian • Religious • Non-Religious • Teen Parents • Gang Members • Athletes • Ignorant People • Racist/Sexist People • Men • Women • Shy People • Drug Users • Others

**In addition, what would you need to do to be an effective leader if there are people with whom you must work who are different than you?**

_____

_____

_____

_____

_____

_____

_____

_____

_____

_____

_____

_____

_____

*If we open a quarrel between the past and the present, we shall find that we have lost the future.*
~Winston Churchill

## Goals:
- To introduce students to various motivational theories & patterns
- To explore "success" and "failure" as motivators
- To encourage students to explore their own motivational techniques and skills for motivating themselves and others

## Class Necessities:
- Student Workbook
- Shoe box (or other small box) filled with 10 pieces of paper crumpled into balls
- Masking Tape
- Clean wastebasket (or painters' 5-gallon tub) into which the paper balls can be thrown
- Classroom chalkboard

## Class Outline:

### Class Activity #1:

At the beginning of class, ask all of the students to leave the room (select a non-disruptive location for them to go!). Tell them that you will either get them one by one, or send another student to get them. Indicate that they are all going to be asked to help with an experiment which will be explained once they are all done.

While the classroom is empty, place three lines of tape on the floor, each at a further distance from the wastebasket or tub. When the room is set up, ask each student to come back to the room, one at a time. (After each student participates, you may have them go to get another student. I have all of the students stay in the room once they have had their turn. It's interesting to debrief how it felt as more and more people started to watch the next person.) Give each student the box of paper balls and tell them to throw as many balls as possible into the wastebasket. Before throwing, they are to select only one distance or point from which they will throw the balls. Be certain to give each person the same instructions and have each student who has already been through the exercise remain silent as each of the others do it.

Record the distance each person stands from the wastebasket. This is the primary point of the exercise, not the number of balls each person throws in. Once everyone has completed their throws, share the results and then debrief/lecture.

# Debrief:

- Ask the students what they think this activity shows? (They'll offer various explanations!)
- What made them select the line that they selected?
- How did it feel to be the first person? Last person?
- How did it feel to have others watching you?
- Any other questions relevant to your group.

# Lecturette:

This exercise is a "non-scientific" way to interpret what motivates a person. This exercise was created to support the research of David McClelland of Harvard University who believes that each person is motivated by one of three orientations — Achievement Oriented; Affiliation-Oriented; or Power-Oriented. Each of the distances relates to one of these motivational patterns.

(Write each orientation on the board/flip chart and explain appropriately)

For those that tossed from the farthest line - This is Power-oriented motivation. These people like power for its own sake or for the benefit of their organization. They like to influence or have impact on people, are attracted by prestigious activities and are sensitive to status and formal recognition. These people enjoy directing others, giving instruction and providing help. Many are seen as Leaders, whether or not they are.

For those that tossed from the middle line - This is Achievement-oriented motivation. These people want to perform better, improve situations, and set their own goals. They like moderate risks and challenging situations. They take personal responsibility for their actions, seek feedback regarding their behavior, and do things in creative, innovative ways. Many are seen as Entrepreneurs. People who selected the middle distance probably have a strong need for achievement. They chose a spot where they (a) had a good chance of landing the balls in the basket, yet (b) the task was still challenging to them.

For those that tossed from the closets line - This is Affiliation-oriented motivation. These people like to interact with others. They enjoy mutual friendships, get involved in group projects, want to be liked and appreciated, enjoy working with others in a cooperative way, and are sensitive to other people's needs. Many are seen as Team workers. People who selected the closest distance are likely to be affiliation-oriented because they wanted to do what they were asked to please the "leader" of the activity.

As you are explaining these behaviors, ask students to comment on whether the description fits them. This provides a segue into the "scientific" research on motivational theory and methods for motivating oneself and others. It is important throughout the lecturette to reconnect the students to the fact that although they may be motivated by one thing, the members of their group may be motivated by other things! Good leaders seek ways to motivate others by what motivates that individual, not only by what motivates the leader.

Prior to class, review the workbook sheets covering Motivation. Depending on your group, you may choose to highlight different aspects of the sheets. The most effective lecturette is given by being very familiar with the sheets, and going through them with the students, stopping for discussion, offering clarification, and asking students for examples in their own lives as they relate.

Be certain to emphasize the differences between "INTRINSIC" and "EXTRINSIC" motivation. One way to do this is to write the words on the board/flip chart and ask the students to give you examples of each. Provide clarification if they have a difficult time. Also, provide examples of how the two factors can be in conflict in a group (describe a leader who is intrinsically motivated trying to lead a group who is extrinsically motivated!).

The sheet on "Success-Achievers" and "Failure-Avoiders" seem to resonate with most students with whom I have worked. This is a very tangible way for them to look at their own motivational styles.

Discuss each of the sheets appropriately, especially asking them about being a Success Achiever or Failure Avoider.

## Class Activity #2:

After going through Maslow's theory and Success & Failure, have each student turn to the page titled "What Motivates Me". Individually, have them rank each of the items on the list, from 1 to 25, with 1 being the most important thing which motivates them, to 25 being the one which motivates them the least.

After they have completed this individually, have the group gather together to discuss what motivates them. Have each student read their top 5 list and their bottom 5 list.Encourage students to listen to one another, especially if they know each other well outside of class, so they can be sensitive to what is motivational to each person. It also promotes the common characteristics that they will see as motivational.

## Debrief:

• What common things did you hear from one another?
• What differences?

- If your top five motivators were taken away from you, how would you motivate yourself?
- How do you communicate to others what motivates you?
- One year ago, were the same things motivating you?  If no, what was and what changed?
- If you hit a wall  trying to reach a goal, what do you do?
- Who helps you be motivated?
- As a leader, how sensitive are you to the needs of others, in terms of what motivates them?
- How do you think your list will change as you get older?
- If you don't know the things which motivate you, how can you learn what they are?
- What would you like to change about how you are motivated?
- What would you like to change about how you motivate others?
- Other questions relevant to your group's experience.

| **Reflection:** | Page 57 or 58 (Alternate) of workbook.

Before you can be motivated or you can help motivate others, there are some things to Before you can understand about motivational theory....

People are typically motivated in one of two ways: **INTRINSICALLY or EXTRINSICALLY**

Intrinsic Motivation means that a person is motivated by something INTERNAL to them, that is, something personal and inside of them (they are motivated by personal success or feeling good about their achievements, etc..). No matter what someone else offers these people, they will only be motivated by their own internal drive.

Extrinsic Motivation means that a person is motivated by things EXTERNAL to them, that is, material goods, money, promotions, recognition. There is not some internal drive for them to achieve their goals, the only way they are motivated is by what someone or something else can give to them.

## Maslow's Hierarchy of Needs

Abraham Maslow, a social scientist, presented theories on how people are driven in addition to the intrinsic and extrinsic ways. He found out that people experience "needs" and when that "need" emerges, it will determine the individual's behavior in terms of motivation, priorities, and action taken.

Maslow's Hierarchy of Needs says that a person needs to take care of lower level needs before they can pass on to the next level of needs. People can also move up and down the levels depending upon the day and/or what is happening in their life. For example, a person can not be motivated to achieve self-expression and fulfillment if they have an empty belly and no roof over his/her head!

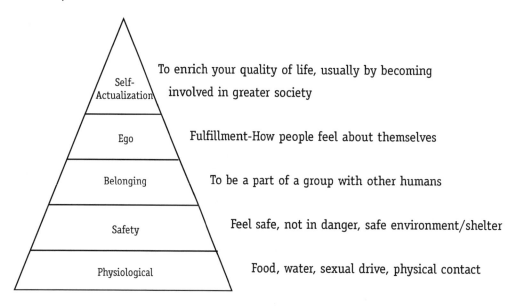

Self-Actualization — To enrich your quality of life, usually by becoming involved in greater society

Ego — Fulfillment-How people feel about themselves

Belonging — To be a part of a group with other humans

Safety — Feel safe, not in danger, safe environment/shelter

Physiological — Food, water, sexual drive, physical contact

# SUCCESS AND FAILURE

People generally fall into one of two categories (although many people can be either depending upon the situation and the consequences associated with success and/or failure):

### *Success Achievers* —
Highly motivated for success. They don't care about failure and in fact, don't pay attention to it. They just want to achieve success. The more success they have, the more motivated they become. The drawback can be that if they do not succeed to the utmost degree, they see this as the same as failure.

### *Examples:*
In classes - striving only for As; Sports teams striving to be #1 and to be seen as "the best"

### *Failure Avoiders* —
Highly motivated because they hate failure. They don't care about success, as long as they don't fail.

### *Examples:*
In classes - satisfied with Ds because at least it's not failing; Sports teams being motivated by a previous loss so that they don't look bad by losing again.

Most of us talk about our own model (that is, what motivates US!) when we talk to others or try to motivate them. For example, if you are a failure avoider, you talk to others that same way.

To cover both ends when you try to motivate others — "It stinks to lose and it's great to win!" "We can't fail and we must win!"

## USING THIS INFORMATION:

• Understand how you are motivated
• Challenge yourself to try a new approach to motivating yourself
  (that is, become a success achiever or failure avoider, if you are the opposite)
• Be aware of how you are approaching situations before you give up!
• Share with others the ways that you are motivated so that they can support and help you
• Avoid "All or Nothing" thinking — it will get in your way!

Rank the following by how much you are motivated by the item listed (1 to 25, with 1 being THE MOST IMPORTANT thing which motivates you, to 25 being THE LEAST IMPORTANT). Rank them all.

_____Good Grades

_____Money

_____Having/Getting a car

_____Having/Getting the approval of my parents

_____Having/Getting the approval of my friends

_____Having a job which pays well

_____Being seen as a good person

_____Food

_____Being able to do things my way

_____Clothes/CDs/Toys

_____Achieving a goal I set for myself

_____Partying/Being social

_____Being Respected

_____Being Noticed

_____Doing the right thing

_____Being responsible (for myself and others)

_____Learning new things

_____Getting a compliment

_____Girls/Guys like me

_____Knowing there may be consequences (good or bad)

_____Having a job which I like

_____Having others look up to me or ask for my advice

_____Having someone to look up to

_____Believing in the "cause"/Standing up for what I believe is right

_____Enjoying what I am doing

### Achievement Motivation:

These people work for the challenge and accomplishment; their challenges will usually be defined internally and may often involve a sense of service to others.

### Hero Motivation:

The main drive is to do well in the eyes of someone admired and sometimes imitated by the person being motivated. The person's interest may be totally in the "hero" (such as a group leader, advisor, teacher, professor, etc.). If the person does not feel that they can achieve the same status as their hero, they may give up on the project or just drop out.

### Affiliation Motivation:

The main motivation is to be in the company of and socialize with other people. These people do best when they can interact with others as they strive toward their goal.

### Competence Motivation:

These people seek job mastery and professional growth. They evaluate every part of their job and they want to be seen as being very good at what they do. They see a job (assignment, project, etc.) as something to be perfected. They will write down much of their work and keep track of their accomplishments because they like to see what they have done.

### Step-Ladder Motivation:

These people are motivated by moving up the ladder. They want to be "top dog" because they see it as a means to a better end. They often are motivated by an underlying agenda or an ulterior motive in mind.

### "Fight for a Cause" Motivation:

These people fight for an issue that they see as very important to their personal values or morals. Their motivation and participation will be very intense and very emotional.

### Power Motivation:

These people seek control. They like to have their individual opinions drive what others will do. In an unsophisticated individual, obnoxiousness and a general overbearing attitude may surface. In a more sophisticated person, obnoxiousness may not appear, but they will not delegate any responsibility or power to other people. The person feels by keeping the information to him/herself that he/she will remain all powerful!

1. Provide low-threat situations that make it easy for others (especially those who are new to the situation, group, or environment) to speak up. Listen to what they are saying.

2. Give others with limited experience and low self-confidence something relatively simple to do at first, or include them in a small-group effort with friendly and experienced models.

3. Look for non-verbal signals (facial expressions, eye contact, posture, tone of voice) that others give you and be responsive to what you see. There is a lot going on non-verbally among people than words alone will tell you.

4. Use people's first names. (Make a habit of remembering them!) Mingle and talk with others as they work. Be generous with positive suggestions and compliments. Let them know you know they are there and tell them you missed them when they are absent.

5. Involve others in setting organizational goals, choosing projects, and discussing issues, using small groups whenever possible.

6. Divide projects into as many manageable parts as possible before asking for volunteers to do the work. Encourage people to seek new experiences rather than asking them to do the same thing over and over again.

7. Get a sense of what people are asking from the organization by spending informal time with them individually and helping them find things to do that match their interests.

8. Involve others in the business of the group or organization itself, to strengthen their sense of "ownership" of the group.

9. Encourage cooperation and teamwork...reward positive interaction and mutual support among people as they work together.

10. Be informal and personable, and get your hands "dirty" once and awhile without getting too deeply involved in details which might limit your perspective of "the big picture."

Participation and involvement represent the most direct line to a person's motivational "buttons." The idea of motivating or "turning on" another person directly is a myth. All you can do is get to know others, manage the structure of the group or organization, encourage a positive atmosphere, and support activities of the group in ways that will give each individual both the will and the opportunity to get involved. Take into consideration all of the things you learned about building a team and apply many of these same concepts to increasing the motivation of others who look to you for leadership!

**People are more productive and motivated when they know...**

- What they are supposed to do

- What authority they have (that is, what they can do without having to "ask" permission)

- How their responsibility relates to the responsibilities of others

- What makes a "job well done!"

- What they are doing exceptionally well

- Where they are falling short

- What they can do to improve

- That they will be rewarded

- That their work has real value

- That you have a sincere concern for them

- That you are anxious for them to succeed in a way that is personally rewarding

**As a Leader...**

- Praise in public, criticize in private

- Be a good listener; listen to all ideas

- Delegate responsibility AND authority to others

- Give credit where credit is due

- Involve others in early stages of decision making

- Show confidence in others; encourage and expect them to do their best

- When you are wrong, admit it!

- Have goals; involve others in setting goals to work towards together

- Remember that people support what they help to create

*Write your thoughts on what motivates you; how you motivate others; and what challenges you face in being motivated (what gets in your way). What did you learn today after ranking the things which are important to keep you motivated?*

_____

_____

_____

_____

_____

_____

_____

_____

_____

_____

_____

_____

_____

_____

_____

_____

_____

*All humankind is divided into three classes:*
*those that are immovable, those that are movable, and those that move.*
~Arab proverb

## Goals:

• To understand the concepts of taking risks (as a leader)—
what makes an appropriate risk; what is a controllable risk;
how does responsibility relate to taking risks; what role "Integrity" plays
when taking risks and making decisions

## Class Necessities:

• Student Workbooks
• "Electric Maze"
• Path through maze (on sheet of paper)
• Digital stopwatch or wristwatch with start/stop
• Masking tape

*(Prior to class)*
*To make an Electric Maze, purchase a 9' x 12' plastic tarp from a painters supply or hardware store. Lay the tarp out flat. Cut in half to create two, 6' x 9' tarps. Starting on one of the 6' edges, at one foot increments, place 1" wide masking tape from end to end, making certain that it is straight prior to pressing to the tarp. Repeat process along the 9' edges until the tarp has 54 boxes (like a tic, tac, toe board only bigger!). (See Maze Wizard key)*

## Class Outline:

Without introducing topic of taking risks as a leader, move all of the chairs and tables out of the way so that you have a large open space

Lay out the "maze" on the floor, with one of the 6 foot edge being laid in a direction to indicate it as the starting edge. Tape the corners so that they do not slip. Make sure that there is plenty of room around the maze. That is, there should be no extra chairs etc. in the way.

You will have to stand on a chair at the other 6 foot edge of the maze to become "The Maze Wizard" (it's easier to see what is going on). Get into role! Let them know that they have a job to do as a group. They must get through the maze...play with them by saying, "Can't you see the path through the maze? It's right there." Indicate that you know the way through because you are the Maze Wizard. You should have a copy of the path in hand, making sure that students cannot see it! (And they will try!)

Their "job" is to get from one end of the maze to the other end. Have the chair at the end facing the end they are starting at (make sense??). (Again, the "ends" should have 6 boxes across)

Standing on your chair, state that only the Maze Wizard sees the path, but as a team they too can make it through. There are a few rules however:

Explain to them, they will have 25 minutes to complete the task. They can use all the time to strategize if they want, but once the first person steps on the maze (whether by choice or accident! so watch), they can no longer communicate verbally. In addition, there can be only one person on the maze at a time (they may point but may not touch the maze without penalty). They also cannot leave "bread crumbs" nor write down clues to their path. Everyone must move through it consecutively (meaning once they make it to a point and make a wrong step, they must RETRACE their steps off the maze, go to the end of their line, and the next person goes). Make sure to keep track that everyone is going through each time.

*The team can lose a minute of time in three ways:*
• If more than one person steps on or touches the maze
• If someone speaks after the first person has stepped on the maze and started
• If, when retracing their steps off of the maze, the person makes a mistake

Allow the group to ask you questions although if they start strategizing with each other, tell them that their time has started. Each time they make a mistake, subtract 1 minute. As they get closer to the end, and if they run out of time, allow them to "negotiate" for more time. Generally, they will negotiate for about 5 minutes extra.

Each time a wrong step is made, you should make a loud "BEEP" sound, indicating that the step is wrong! (get into it!). Make sure that the person retraces their steps off of the maze!!!! This is often where they lose the most time. Participants will insist that when they are just "testing" a box that it doesn't count as a full step. The issue of "integrity" therefore becomes significant in this activity and is powerful to address during debriefing.

Have all of the students stay at the starting end so that you can clearly see what is going on. As they get farther through the maze, they will move around the edges and to the other end as they "guide" each other through, this is okay. Watch their steps so that you are sure when they make a mistake and when they are correct. They will frequently step on the same (wrong) boxes several times, thinking that they have not stepped on them!

OBSERVE WHAT TAKES PLACE WITH THE GROUP THROUGH THIS ACTIVITY
SO THAT YOU CAN FOCUS ON DIFFERENT THINGS DURING DEBRIEFING.

## Debrief:

- What happened in this activity?  What do you think it's messages were?
  (They should say things like communication, teamwork, trust, setting a goal, etc.)
- How about risk-taking?  You had all the time to strategize, but eventually, someone had to just get on! (Have them talk about their strategy and the risk-taking issue)
- How different did this look when you were in the middle of the maze versus on the outside?
- How did people take on different leadership roles?
- How did it feel when you made a mistake?  How about when others made a mistake?
- What about the things for which you lost time?  What was the same about these?
  (Talk about "controllable risks"- they got penalized for things which they could control if they paid attention. They also should "learn from their mistakes" when retracing)
- How was the issue of integrity dealt with by the group?  For example, when a step was incorrect or a full step was not taken into a box but the turn continued, how did the group respond?  How does this relate to real-life risk taking and leadership?  If no one is "watching" when you take a step, does it really count? (It would be unusual that this would not arise as an issue for the group).
- Any other questions which you think should be raised....including, how does this relate to real life activities  as student leaders?  What have they learned?

*Discuss further the issue of Risk and decision making as leadership concepts, not just "taking risks" in life. Use "Taking Risks" worksheet.*

- Why is it so hard to take risks as a leader? (talk about responsibility for the consequences)
- What role does experimenting and learning from mistakes/successes play in leadership?
- What is the role of communication when you as a leader want to take a risk for your group (or if you want to get your group to take a risk)
- "Do it; Fix it; Try it Again" - write this on the board and discuss what it means to them; see if they can give  appropriate examples
- Think of "Enabling Others to Act" from their leadership profile—it says to plan "little wins"; how does this relates to taking risks?
- Talk about Low-Risk, Medium-Risk, and High-Risk decisions as a leader—have them share examples.

Have them close their eyes (this takes some prodding!). Get them to relax and then describe that they should imagine that they are taking a risk that they have wanted to take. This may be a major change in life; standing up for a belief; sharing something important to someone who is special to them, etc. Ask them to focus on the FEELING of taking the risk. What does it make them think of, what emotion comes up? Fear, excitement, curiosity, hope, etc. (list a variety of emotions, slowly). When they are ready, have them open their eyes. They are to write about the "risk"—what do they want to do? What does it feel like to do it? What will convince them to do it? How will it feel when they take this risk? Etc.

Page 60 or 61 (Alternate) of workbook.

# "Maze Wizard" Key

(You can create your own key!  Blackened boxes are path through)

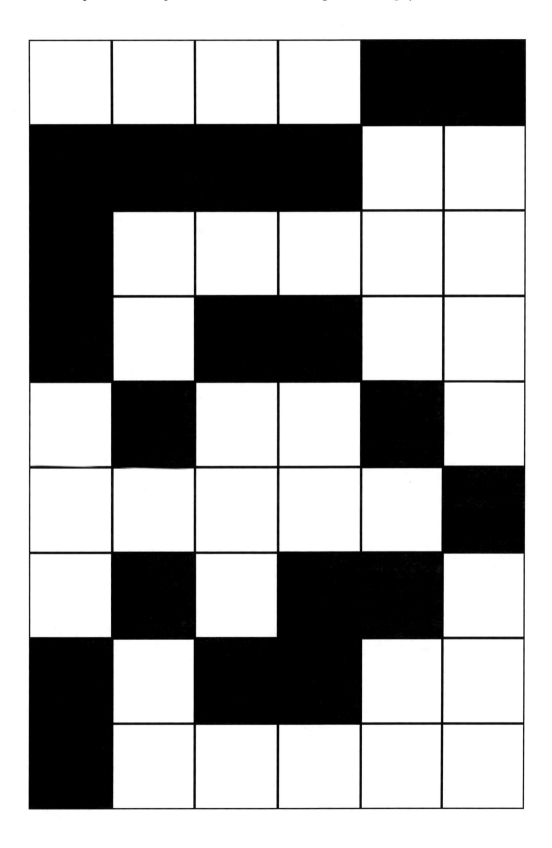

Taking risks is a big part of being a leader...
Risk-taking as a leader can be different than taking risks in your daily life:

Experimenting • Learning from Mistakes & Successes • Trying Again

*There are different approaches:*
• Innovation
• Risking Failure
• Setting up little Experiments

**Think of leadership Risk Taking as "DOING IT — FIXING IT — TRYING IT AGAIN"**

Risk Taking also involves making decisions based on what the consequences may be:

# Types of Decisions

*Routine Decisions:*    Simple in nature with LOW risks.
                    "What am I going to wear today?"
                    "What am I going to eat for dinner?"

*Adaptive Decisions:*    Involves needing to make adjustments in a plan or existing
                    decision due to outside factors or forces. The risk is MEDIUM.

"Getting a flat tire riding your bike home from work..."
"You are running late for school and are not sure what to do to prevent getting an absence."

*Creative Decisions:*    Involves a major change that you will have to live with.  There
                    is a HIGH consequence of risk and error.
                    "Marriage, moving, job change, school change, etc."
                    "Any major life decisions..."

*Decision Making Involves:*
1.    Consideration of human & material resources (either of yourself or of your group)
2.    Judgment (the ability to be logical and objective)
3.    Prioritizing
4.    Taking responsibility for your decision
5.    Directing (identifying the next step)

*Following the guided imagery, write your reflections on what risk you want to take and what it could feel like to take your risk, as well as, how you will know when you are ready to do it.*

_____

_____

_____

_____

_____

_____

_____

_____

_____

_____

_____

_____

_____

_____

_____

_____

_____

_____

*There are only two mistakes one can make along the road to truth:*
*1) not going all the way; and 2) not starting.*
*~Buddha*

## Goals:
- To introduce students to the concept of creative thinking in their role as leaders
- To promote working with others & to "break out of the box"
- To encourage dialogue on how creative thinking is necessary to be successful as leaders

## Class Necessities:

- Student Workbook
- Raw eggs - Enough for each group of three to have one, plus a few extras just in case!
- Plastic straws (with or without paper wrapping) - Enough for each group of three to have twenty (20)
- Masking tape - Enough for each group of three to have one thirty (30) inch piece
- Several large plastic garbage bags

## Class Outline:

Without introducing the topic of Creative Thinking, split into groups of three. Encourage them to work with someone they have not necessarily worked with in a small group.

Create the scene by stating that NASA is looking for a very talented team to hire who are capable of creating a protective contraption to get an egg through the atmosphere and landing without breaking. Each team is given limited resources and must create the contraption with ONLY these resources. This includes the egg; they must be very careful and gentle with it because these are limited items! They cannot use scissors, clippers, lighters (there's always one who pulls it out clandestinely!), etc. because this would constitute a violation of integrity. They have the first half of class period (your call) to complete their contraption.

While you are talking, pull a chair out into the middle of the room and stand upon it while explaining: To prove that your contraption will work, it must be dropped from approximately 6 feet off the ground and must survive the fall. If there is a tie, the contraptions will be dropped from higher distances.

Remind them that NASA is not skilled enough to predict the atmosphere and to have something reenter it and land ON a target, therefore their contraption must be AROUND their egg, not on the ground for it to land. Other than this GIVE THEM NO CLUES, however encourage them to be creative! The only facilitation you need to do is to walk around, keep them on task, and be time keeper.  Also, encourage them to use each other's brain, especially if one of the group members is not working or talking or otherwise contributing.

When they are ready to present their contraption, they must give their team name and the name of their contraption, and "sell" the contraption to the class.  Before they drop, make sure that you put down the large trash bag - I usually cut out the seams, spread it out, and tape the edges a little.

## Debrief:

- Discuss what this activity had to do with Leadership? (Ask them to brainstorm what they needed to complete  the projects?)
- How many don't think they are creative or have heard that creativity is for art class?
- How can a leader be creative when their organization has limited resources or the boundaries/rules are limiting?
- What are some examples of creative problem solving in which they have participated in their own lives?
- How does creative thinking pull together all of the things we have discussed and learned this quarter about leadership and being a leader?

During debrief, go over the pages in the book and explain each concept.  Have students brainstorm examples as appropriate.

With "Fifty Excuses" encourage them to listen for when others (or themselves) say these things and recognize that this is a "flag" that creativity may be lacking in their project and/or objective.

Creative Thinking is not a natural process. In fact it is very unnatural. Our brain is a powerful self-organizing system and creative thinking allows us to break traditional thinking and generate new ideas!

## Ten Mental "Locks" that Hinder Creativity

Roger Von Oech, a well-known speaker and presenter on creative thinking, has identified ten mental locks that block our ability to be innovative. He believes that if people are aware of these mental locks, then they can attempt to UNLOCK them to become more creative. The ten "deadly" locks to creativity:

1. **Looking for The Right Answer** - Have you ever considered that there might be several other answers that might be just as correct and right as the first "right" answer you came up with? Attempting to find the "right" answer hinders our ability to look beyond the obvious and explore other possibilities. Von Oech encourages us to look for the second and third "right" answers.

2. **That's Not Logical** - Looking at your answers logically is helpful if you're in the practical phase of evaluating your ides, but it has no business affecting the general phase of creative thinking when you're brainstorming for possible solutions. The use of metaphor - linking two ideas together - can be a helpful but illogical way of being creative.

3. **Following the Rules** - It's important that you open yourself up to as many options as possible to come up with creative ideas. You might find yourself breaking out of one pattern to discover another which will allow for greater imagination and creativity. If we are simply generating ideas, then what need do we have to "follow the rules?" This is a mental lock because it means that we can only think of things as they are and not as they may be!

4. **Being Practical** - Too many people get caught up in "what-is" instead of "what-if." Allow yourself to be impractical, looking at alternative ideas, as stepping stones to possible ideas and solutions.

5. **Avoiding Ambiguity** - Working on a task in which you were given specific instructions doesn't allow you to utilize your imagination. Welcome ambiguity (being vague!) and see it as an opportunity to search for the possible idea. Being ambiguous gives more freedom to the person working on the problem which in turn allows for greater creativity.

6. **Believing that To Err is Wrong** - Making mistakes communicates to us that we are being innovative and not afraid to take that path which is less traveled. Making mistakes allows us to learn what doesn't work, and also gives us the opportunity to try a different approach. Let us all learn that we should not penalize people for failing because it hinders our ability to take risks and try new things.

7. **Believing that Play is Frivolous** - Nonsense! Some of our best ideas come when we're not working, but playing. For some, being creative occurs most easily in a relaxed, unstructured environment when we are having fun. Fun is a great motivator of excellent ideas.

8. **Thinking "That's Not My Area"** - Individuals should be challenged to hunt for ideas. We should always be on the lookout for exciting and new ideas. We limit our scope of looking for ideas, then we risk not being as diversified and knowledgeable as we could be.

9. **Avoiding Being Foolish** - Let your hair down and encourage others to be creative and fun thinkers! Coming up with wild ideas may not be initially helpful, but they could spark some creative thinking in someone else. The best way to get along is to go along with whatever is happening, even if that means being foolish.

10. **Thinking "I'm not Creative"** - Often what we think has a way of becoming true. Encourage each other to believe in themselves and their ability to come up with ideas. Believing in yourself allows you to take risks, discover new ways of thinking, and developing creative ideas. Winners are winners because they believe themselves to be, but losers usually have a reason or an excuse to allow themselves to lose.

*Summarized from* <u>A Whack on the Side of the Head,</u> *by Roger Von Oech*

# Groups also find reasons NOT TO creatively problem solve...

### Problem-Solving:
Changing things from the way they are to the way you want them to be.

### Creativity:
Combining old thing in new ways or new things in old ways.

# Thing which keep groups from being creative:

### Group Think -
Conforming to existing ideas, suggestions, leadership, etc. A bunch of "yes" people.

### Abilene Paradox-
When group members agree to do something, even though nobody wants to do it, just because each perceives that everyone else wants to do it.

### Trained Incapacities -
Self-imposed limitations which come from failed trials.

One of your roles as a leader is to provide strategies and promote creativity and creative problem-solving in your organization, rather than accepting things as they are!

People who want to avoid having to do things differently or to change have a million reasons!

1. We tried that before.
2. Our school is different.
3. It costs too much
4. That's beyond our responsibility
5. We're all too busy to do that.
6. That's not my job.
7. It's too radical a change.
8. We don't have the time.
9. Not enough help.
10. Our school is too small.
11. We don't have the resources.
12. Not practical for busy people.
13. The students will never buy it.
14. We've never done it before.
15. It's against policy.
16. Runs up our costs.
17. We don't have the authority.
18. That's too intellectual and above us.
19. We did all right without it.
20. That's what to expect from staff.
21. It's never been tried before.
22. Let's form a committee to figure it out.
23. Has anyone else tried it?
24. I don't see the connection.
25. It won't work.
26. Let's get back to reality.
27. That's not our problem.
28. Why? It is still working today.
29. I don't like the idea.
30. You're all right, but...
31. You're two years ahead.
32. We're not ready for that.
33. We don't have equipment or room.
34. We don't have the people for it.
35. It isn't in the budget.
36. Can't teach an old dog new tricks!
37. Good thought, but impractical.
38. Let's come back to it.
39. Let's give it more thought.
40. Put it in writing.
41. They'll laugh at us.
42. Not that again.
43. Where'd you dig that one up?
44. What you're really saying is...
45. With your friends, yes; mine, no!
46. Let's all sleep on it.
47. I know a friend who tried it.
48. Too much trouble to change.
49. We've always done it this way.
50. It's impossible.

### Goals:
• To bring the class experience to closure and to provide students and opportunity to establish a "vision" for themselves
• To celebrate success and the team which has developed (hopefully!) through the class experience
• To provide students reflective time to assess what they have discovered about their leadership skills
• To provide students the opportunity to give feedback to facilitator  (evaluation of class)

## Class Necessities:

• Plain white envelopes (business size)
• Designer paper (paper with designs)
• Food or any other class selection for celebrating!

## Class Outline:

Pass out an envelope to each student.  Have each student select a piece of paper of their choice. After summarizing (briefly) your observations of their growth or development as leaders and individuals (hopefully!), indicate that this is now their chance to set some goals or a "vision" for themselves for the next year.

Have them address the envelope to themselves, at the address where they will be certain to receive mail (either in person or forwarded).  On the piece of paper, they are to write a letter to themselves which they will receive ONE YEAR from the date they are writing it.  Make sure that they put the date on the letter.  Encourage them to write their goals and expectations of themselves in one year, either leadership related or in general to life.  Perhaps they are facing a difficult decision and they want to check in on themselves.  Let them know that you will not read the letter; they are to write it, fold it, and seal it into the envelope.  Encourage them to think about what they want to write rather than just writing "hi".

Writing the letter typically takes 15 - 20 minutes.  I often allow additional time because the group will like to share things that they have learned about themselves and highlight new expectations or goals they have for themselves.

Once the letters are completed and sealed, collect them.  Make certain that you put a sticky note or other notation on them so that you remember when to mail them the following year!

Use the remainder of class to gather an evaluation of the class. You may have a method which you prefer. It is important to get feedback from the students, both for improving the class and "molding" it to your particular students. In addition, it assists you in modeling the way for the students, indicating that there are things which are your strengths as well as your challenge areas.

I also take this time to encourage students who are interested in further studying leadership and putting it into action, to consider a more advanced class. The Advanced Leadership class I offer is a time for students to conduct Community Leadership Projects (CLPs) of their choice. They also learn to incorporate the skills they have learned through Leadership 101 in a more significant way. You may consider doing something similar, that is, offering an upper level class. If you are stumped, feel free to contact me for additional activities and formats for an advanced class.

This final class is also an outstanding time to celebrate as a group. Food is usually how my students choose to celebrate. At times, the SCRABBLE® game comes out, and I break the class into teams, to play "Leadership Scrabble". Same rules as SCRABBLE®, except every word must relate to leadership. The group must determine when they will accept a word, and it is permissible to make the team with the word explain (in detail, for the questionable ones!) how the word relates to leadership.

Enjoy the role you have in contributing to the education and development of young leaders (and young people in general) who should be more confident, self-assured, comfortable standing up for themselves, and willing to take on leadership roles, after completing this class!

# Appendix

_____  Stand up for what I believe.

_____  Confront members of my club, team, or organization, and my friends on inappropriate comments and behavior.

_____  When I am 18, I will register to vote and vote!

_____  Nominate a friend to run for a position of leadership in my school or community.

_____  Run for a position on student council or other club.

_____  Find out which school committees have positions available for students and step up to serve in that role.

_____  Attend a meeting or activity sponsored by a club or organization I typically donít attend.

_____  Set high academic standards for myself and strive to achieve them.

_____  Set high goals and expectations for myself and strive to achieve them, even if others aren't behind me!

_____  Refuse to participate in a school or club event that is not a positive representation of my school or community, even if my friends are pressuring you to participate.

_____  Invite local political candidates to a meeting of my student council to present their views and platform.  Engage in a discussion with the candidates.

_____  Write a letter to the editor on a topic for which I feel strongly.  Do my homework on the subject and prove it by the content of my letter.

_____  Write a list of issues I feel strongly about and identify clubs, organizations, or volunteer activities that can help me develop this interest.

_____  Attend a controversial event or speaker in your community and write a personal reflection  on the event.  Discuss the topic/event with a friend who holds the opposing view- donít try to convince him/her to my "side" — simply discuss.

_____  Attend a student council meeting, even if Iím not a member.  Offer to work on one of the committees.

_____  Attend a community rally or parade promoting peace and justice in my community or school.

_____  I will not use drugs and alcohol even if others are pressuring me to use.

_____ Attend any meetings related to the future of my school or school district. Participate in focus groups or discussion on school policies and priorities.

_____ I will write a personal ìvisionî and strive to achieve my vision.

_____ Have my club or team write a ìvisionî and make that vision a daily way to achieve the goals of my group.

_____ Share my hopes, expectations, and dreams with my friends and family.

_____ I will volunteer for activities which move my school and community forward in a positive way.

_____ Tell others why you choose to be a leader and what it means to you.

_____ Get a mentor or be a mentor to other students or kids in the community.

_____ Be a positive force in my school — whether in a class, as a volunteer, on a team, or with a club.

_____ When new policies are put into action, I will help others see why the policy will work.

_____ I will respect that members of my organization or team have other involvements which are important to them and I will support them with these.

_____ If the place where I work is looking for new employees, I will let others know.

_____ I will strive to develop strong and sincere friendships with others. I will meet new people and try different things with them.

_____ As a leader, I will remember the power I have as a role model to others and will behave appropriately.

_____ Tutor an elementary student or another child in my neighborhood.

_____ Volunteer at a homeless shelter, food bank, or other community agency and invite my friends or organization to do the same.

_____ When my peers complain about something they do not like or know about, I will help them find out information about that issue and encourage them to take action. When the status quo is harmful to others, I will help others take a stand.

_____ Publicly recognize the successes of other teams, clubs, or people.

_____ Recognize the unique talents of each member of my organization or peer group. Encourage them to share these with my group or have the group tap into them for projects.

_____ Commit to the rules of our school or group and help others to act with integrity.

_____ Offer to help a friend or classmate on a project or issues that is important to her/him.

_____ Help show a new student or teacher around school.  Or invite a new neighbor to do something with me and my friends.

_____ Invite someone who is normally quiet to participate in a club activity or discussion in class.

_____ Coach a little league team or youth soccer team.  Encourage others to help me.

_____ Participate in a city-wide sports team even if I am on a team with others I don't know.

_____ Serve as a spokesperson for your club, organization, or team to others at school or in the community, for an issue which is important to your community.

_____ Help my parents or teachers or club on a project without complaining about the time commitment.

_____ Plan an activity with my organization which showcases the talents of our members.

_____ Offer to "buddy" with a younger student at our school and help ease their transition  from middle school (or junior high) to high school.

_____ Volunteer at a homeless shelter or food bank, and invite my friends or organization to do the same.

_____ Have my team, club, organization, or work collect canned foods at the holidays to donate to a local food bank.

_____ Dedicate myself to my leadership action plan and be the support person for someone else for their leadership action plan.

_____ Sit next to a student who needs a little extra help in a class and be the one to offer help.

_____    As a member of my team, I will show up to practice on time and prepared.

_____    As a member of my student government, I will show up on time to meetings.

_____    Sit in the front row in your classes.

_____    Attend and speak up at "Shared Decision Making" or
"School Improvement" Meeting.

_____    Attend a school board meeting.

_____    When one of your classes has a substitute teacher, offer to show him/her
around and help with difficult situations during the class.
Do not be one of the students to "pick on the new guy."

_____    Set standards of behavior for in school, in the community, with
my friends, or with my family which allow me to be considered
a role model to others.

_____    Develop a personal "Honor Code" for my academic projects and exams.
I will sign it on all of my work to show my standards. If I am a member of a
club, team, or other organization, we will all develop the Honor Code and
will sign it on our work.

_____    I will speak for myself and encourage others to do the same.
I will use "I" statements.

_____    I will follow through on my commitments. I will "walk the talk" of a leader.

_____    Treat others the way I want to be treated.

_____    Participate in school and community activities which make
things better for others.

_____    Run for a position on student council. Volunteer for or apply for
a position on a school or community committee.

_____    Stay true to my personal values, even when peer pressure tries
to make me do things which are destructive to myself and others.

_____    Balance my lifestyle and goals as a person and leader. As a student, I will
work to balance my academics, clubs & athletics, community service, work,
and commitment to my family and friends. When I am overwhelmed, I will
be the one to say "no" and will not over-commit.

_____    Respect, value, and share my culture and background.
Respect, value, and share the culture and background of others.

_____ Publicly thank my favorite teachers and coaches for what they do.

_____ Attend the plays, musical performances, art exhibits, athletic events, etc. of my friends and family.

_____ Send congratulation cards to my friends or other important people in my life for their successes.

_____ Send congratulation cards to my friends who are graduating or going to college.

_____ Acknowledge the milestones of my friends and families (anniversaries, birthdays, new jobs, Mother's Day, Father's Day, etc.). Help them recognize the importance of the events in our lives.

_____ Recognize and support the involvements of my fellow team or club members beyond our group.

_____ Write a thank you to a friend who helped me on a project or task.

_____ Nominate a friend, mentor, or family member for one of many community awards. Do something special for them whether or not they get the award.

_____ Take a favorite teacher, counselor, boss, or coach to lunch and share why I appreciate or admire him/her.

_____ Participate in an activity sponsored by an organization with which I typically don't hang out.

_____ Plan a fun and relaxing surprise activity for my friends and I as a study break during finals.

_____ Volunteer my time at a nursing home. If my grandparents are no longer living, I can "adopt a grandparent".

_____ I will support fellow members of my organization in a difficult situation and will find things in the situation to keep us optimistic.

_____ Spend extra time with a younger child in my neighborhood.

_____ Share with my parents, sister/brother, friends, etc. something for which I am really proud of them.

## Other Ways | I Can Take Action

**Challenging the Process:**

_____    _____

_____    _____

_____    _____

**Inspiring a Shared Vision:**

_____    _____

_____    _____

_____    _____

**Enabiling Others to Act:**

_____    _____

_____    _____

_____    _____

**Modeling the Way:**

_____    _____

_____    _____

_____    _____

**Encouraging the Heart:**

_____    _____

_____    _____

_____    _____

## Leadership Action Plan

My leadership goal is:

_____

_____

_____

The first action I will take to achieve this goal is:

_____

_____

_____

The people who will help or support me are:

_____

_____

_____

The things or people which (who) may get in my way are:

_____    _____    _____

I will be ready to deal with these things by:

_____

_____

_____

I will know I have achieved my goal when:

_____

_____

I will check my progress on the following dates:

_____    _____    _____

This goal will be accomplished by the following date: _____

The following sample class schedule is based upon a nine week quarter, with classes being 90 minutes long, two times a week. There is one "open" day built in, and although it is at the end of the quarter, this is simply included somewhere in the schedule to provide flexibility with school requirements (testing, in-service days, canceled school days, etc.). In addition, issues may come up in your group which demand flexibility with your class planning and need to be addressed in a timely manner. Clearly, your open schedule may come up sooner in your quarter!

If you are on a 50-minute, three-times-a-week schedule, modify this schedule appropriately. You can determine necessary alterations to class plans in advance and break the activities up as needed. As mentioned earlier in the guide, debriefing for some of the activities is extremely important to be done at the time of the activity, which should be considered when altering your schedule.

**Week One**
| | |
|---|---|
| I. | Introduction/Defining Leadership |
| II. | Qualities of Leadership/What Makes A Good Leader |

**Week Two**
| | |
|---|---|
| III. | Leadership Practices Inventory |
| IV. | X/Y Theories/Power/Influence (may be continued to Class V) |

**Week Three**
| | |
|---|---|
| V. | Communication & Listening |
| VI. | Consensus/Negotiation/Conflict Management |

**Week Four**
| | |
|---|---|
| VII. | Ethical Decision Making |
| VIII. | Team Building |

**Week Five**
| | |
|---|---|
| IX. | Midterm/Present Organizational Observations |
| X. | Gender Differences in Leadership (Modern/Traditional) |

**Week Six**
| | |
|---|---|
| XI. | Tolerance/Diversity and Leadership (Session One) |
| XII. | Tolerance/Diversity and Leadership (Session Two) |

**Week Seven**
| | |
|---|---|
| XIII. | Motivation |
| XIV. | Risk Taking, Decision Making, & Integrity |

Week Eight

Week Nine

The purpose of this class is to introduce you to the concepts of personal development and leadership. It will:

- provide a basic understanding of leadership concepts, theories, and group dynamics;
- assist you in developing a personal philosophy of leadership;
- determine an awareness of one's own ability and style of leadership;
- provide the opportunity to develop essential leadership skills through study, discussion, and observation.

In addition to regular attendance and participation, the following assignments/ projects will comprise the grading for this class:

## Reflection Papers:

There will be one (1) or two (2) reflection papers due each week. The Reflection Questions are in the workbook. The papers should be no less than one full page. There are some class topics for which reflections will not be assigned.

## Organizational Observation:

Select and attend a meeting of an organization with which you are not familiar. Observe the group dynamics, the "leader's" style, and the outcome of the meeting. Write a one to two page observation paper identifying the strengths of the organization, the challenges (observed) and offer suggestions for improvements. Examples include a city council meeting, staff meeting of an organization, student organization meeting, athletic team meeting, etc. Be certain to get permission to attend the meeting as needed. (A suggested outline to help you with your observation will be given to you by the teacher.)

## Leader Research Paper:

Select a biography or autobiography (at least one book must be used) and write a three to five (3-5) page paper summarizing the person's style of leadership and reflecting on the leader's impact on society. You should describe the circumstances which have impacted this person to make them who they are, and to highlight both the positive and negative aspects in their styles (all leaders have some of both!). Be certain to identify what profession or field in which this person has the greatest leadership influence. Include your references in the paper. ENCYCLOPEDIAS (whether a book or from computer) should be used as supplemental resources. This is not a book report, but an analysis of a leadership style. By mid-terms you must select the person and book you will be using. The paper is due during finals week.

## Exams:

There are two exams - a mid-term and a final. These will give you the opportunity to synthesize ideas and philosophies regarding leadership.

1. What is the nature of the group?
   - describe the organization (briefly)
   - what is the organization's purpose?
   - who are members?

2. Procedures:
   - how does the group determine its tasks, agenda, etc.?
   - how are decisions made?
   - are the members all involved?

3. Structure:
   - who leads, controls, influences the group (whether officially or unofficially)?
   - how does the "informal" structure affect the "formal" structure?

4. Communication:
   - were people clearly expressing their ideas?
   - did everyone understand what was going on during the meeting?
   - did members ask a lot of questions (as if they did not understand things)?
   - what "non-verbal" messages did you observe?
   - did anyone seem to be pushing their own ideas/causes and excluding others?

5. Group Dynamics:
   - did the group work together?
   - were people interested or disinterested in the workings of the group?
   - was their a united feeling about decisions?

6. Atmosphere:
   - describe the atmosphere of the meeting (warm, friendly, cool, hostile, etc.)?
   - did the atmosphere seem different at different times or when certain people spoke?
   - were opposing views or negative feelings expressed?
   - were members willing to share their personal feelings?

7. Other observations:
   - who talks, how often, how long?
   - to whom do speakers look? how often?
   - do speakers project their voices? mumble?
   - anything else that you observed that you think is relevant?

8. Summary:
   - Think about the group process & make suggestions/comments on:
   - ways in which the group could improve its productivity?
   - do you feel the group is effective? why? why not?
   - what recommendations could you make to the leader to assist them in working with this organization?
   - what you would do differently if you were the leader of this organization?

Examples of Leaders to read and write about...this is a very short list (and in no particular order!). If you are interested in someone, talk with me to confirm your choice prior to researching the person. Your selected person does not need to be on this list, these are only suggestions and come from the people students have done their papers on in the past:

| | | | |
|---|---|---|---|
| Fidel Castro | Toni Morrison | Abraham Lincoln | Winston Churchill |
| William Shakespeare | Rigoberta Menchu | Golda Mier | Rita Moreno |
| Mahatma Ghandi | Robert Bruce | Ralph Nader | Rush Limbaugh |
| Reba MacIntyre | Winnemucca | Benito Mussolini | Bill Clinton |
| Bill Gates | Quincy Jones | Harvey Milk | John Lennon |
| Julia Child | Billy Jean King | Arthur Ashe | Ansel Adams |
| Mick Jagger | Elvis Presley | Marianne Williamson | Hillary Clinton |
| Karl Marx | Dan Marino | Eleanor Roosevelt | Malcolm X |
| Marilyn Monroe | Oprah Winfrey | Joseph Stalin | Brett Butler |
| Michael Jordan | Louis Farrakhan | Carrie Nation | John F. Kennedy |
| Pablo Picasso | Susan B. Anthony | Maya Angelou | Edward James Olmos |
| Sigmund Freud | Jesse Jackson | Colin Powell | Margaret Thatcher |
| Martin Luther King, Jr. | Wilma Mankiller | Cesar Chavez | Nelson Mandella |
| Adolph Hitler | Jimi Hendrix | Barbra Streisand | Harriet Tubman |
| Crazy Horse | Dian Fossey | Magic Johnson | Al Capone |
| Tori Amos | Steve Jobs | Baby Doe Tabor | Abigal Adams |

**Remember —** a leader is not always affable (well-liked by all), and yet can be effective in demonstrating "leadership."

## Your paper should highlight such things as the following:

- Describe what the person's life was/is like.
- What has occurred to make her/him the person s/he is now.
- Describe the person's style of leadership — Why do people view this person as a leader?
- How was this person motivated to become a leader? Was there a significant incident which occurred or did the person end up a leader as a haphazard result of life?
- How has the person effected society? Keep the person in perspective — most (not all) individuals have good and bad parts about their personalities — even the "best" leaders.
- Include factual information & also include "subjective" assessment of the person as a leader (that is, include your opinion as to why you believe the person is a leader).
- Include your references — the book (s) & resources that you used for your paper. This includes the name of the book (s), the authors, publisher, & the year it was published.

**Remember —** this is not simply a book report, it is your evaluation of a leader's life based on the autobiography or biography that you read. It should not simply summarize information from an encyclopedia! Preferably, your paper should be TYPED, DOUBLE-SPACED, and will be 3-5 pages minimum.

For this test, you should take your time to complete your answers. Responses should be in FULL sentences. Points will be taken off for poor spelling. You may use dictionaries if necessary. Please write your answers on the attached paper. This exam is worth 100 points.

1. Select one of the five behavior descriptions of The Leadership Challenge and describe a situation where you saw it in practice (either by yourself or by someone else). Be specific:
   • Challenging the Process
   • Inspiring a Shared Vision
   • Enabling Others to Act
   • Modeling the Way
   • Encouraging the Heart

2. **Part A.** Describe what you see as the challenge & role for a leader to bring a group to consensus, especially when members have diverse views & "competing" roles.
   **Part B.** In what situations is it more appropriate to use "Majority Rule"? In what situations is it more appropriate to use "Consensus"?

3. **Part A.** Describe the differences of "X" people and "Y" people
   **Part B.** Describe the differences between an "Abdicratic leader"; "Democratic leader"; and "Autocratic leader."
   **Part C.** What are the differences between "Group-Centered Leadership" and "Leader-Centered Leadership?"

4. **Part A.** What characteristics make a "good" communicator and listener?
   **Part B.** Describe how a leader can strengthen her/his communication skills.

5. Describe the similarities and differences of POWER, INFLUENCE, and AUTHORITY, and explain how a leader can use each in a positive and negative way (whether with a small group or with broader society). (Do not use the words to describe the words!)

6. Describe one ethical dilemma which you believe young adults face today. How do Kitchener's 5 requirements for an ethical decision impact how they deal with the dilemma? [Autonomy; Doing No Harm; Benefiting Others; Being Just; Being Faithful (Loyal)]

7. Think of the various ways and characteristics we have looked at while defining leadership. What is your personal definition of leadership and how consistently do you behave similar to your definition?

For this test, you should take your time to complete your answers. Responses should be in FULL sentences. Points will be taken off for poor spelling. You may use dictionaries if necessary. Please write your answers on the attached paper. This exam is worth 100 points.

1. Research has shown that there are Traditional (or "masculine") and Modern (or "feminine") styles of leading and communicating. Describe two (2) examples of these differences (meaning, two Traditional styles and two Modern styles). Remember, we discussed that both men and women can carry out either style.

2. **Part A.** Why is it so difficult to take risks, especially when you are in a leadership role? What must you consider when taking risks as a leader?
   **Part B.** How do you encourage yourself to be a risk taker when you are in a leadership role?

3. Define "Integrity" in your own words. How does it apply to individuals who are seen as leaders? (Do not use a dictionary for this one!)

4. Describe a time in your life when you solved a difficult problem through creative thinking. Be specific and complete.

5. **Part A.** Describe three (3) characteristics necessary to develop a strong "team."
   **Part B.** What role do you generally play when you are a member of the team (examples leader, follower, visionary, decision maker, etc.) and is this role consistent with who you are? (That is, would you prefer to play a different role?)

6. The issue of "diversity" (people coming from different cultures, races, classes, genders, religions, beliefs, etc.) is important in our society today. Put yourself in a leadership position and explain how you would deal with the differences people bring to groups and how you would manage the conflicts which can arise from these differences.

7. Based upon what you have learned this quarter, what advice would you give to others who are (or want to become) student leaders?

8. How have your thoughts and definitions of "leadership" (the word, not the class!) changed from the beginning of the quarter to now? Be specific.

Casse, Pierre (1982). Training for the multicultural manager. Washington, DC: Society of Intercultural Education [Out of Print]

Forbess-Greene, Susan (1983). The encyclopedia of icebreakers: Structured activities that warm up, motivate, challenge, acquaint and energize. San Diego, CA: University Associates.

Gilligan, Carol (1982). In a different voice. Cambridge, MA: Harvard University Press.

Kohlberg's stages of moral development. In Crain, T. (1992). Theories of development: Concepts and applications (3rd Edition). Englewood Cliffs, NJ: Prentice-Hall, Inc.

Kouzes, James, & Posner, Barry (1987). The leadership challenge: How to get extraordinary things done in organizations. San Francisco: Jossey-Bass, Inc.

Kouzes Posner International    15419 Banyan Lane    Monte Sereno, CA 95030
Phone/FAX    408.354.9170

McGregor, Douglas (1985). The human side of enterprise (25th Anniversary edition). New York: McGraw Hill.

PBS Video Collection 1320 Braddock Place Alexandria, VA  22314 1.800.344.3337

Peters, Tom (1994). The pursuit of wow: Every person's guide to topsy turvy times. New York: Vintage Books.

Project Adventure, Incorporated:
| | | | |
|---|---|---|---|
| P.O. Box 100 | Hamilton, MA  01936 | 508/468-7981 | FAX  508/468-7605 |
| P.O. Box 2447 | Covington, GA  30209 | 404/784-9310 | FAX  404/787-7764 |
| 116 Maple Street | Brattleboro, VT  05301 | 802/254-5054 | FAX  802/254-5182 |
| P.O. Box 14171 | Portland, OR  97214 | 503/239-0168 | FAX  503/236-6765 |

Rohnke, Karl. (1984). Silver bullets: A guide to initiative problems, adventure games and trust activities. Dubuque, IA: Kendall/Hunt Publishing Company.

Rohnke, Karl (1989). Cowstails and cobras II: A guide to games, initiatives, ropes courses, and adventure curriculum. Dubuque, IA: Kendall/Hunt Publishing Company.

Schaef, Anne Wilson (1981). Women's reality: An emerging female system in a white male society. San Francisco: Harper & Company.

Von Oech, Roger (1993). A whack on the side of the head. New York: Warner Books, Inc.

*The future is here, we are it, we are on our own.*
~Bob Weir

*The world is round and the place that may seem like the end*
*may also be the beginning.*
~Ivy Baker Priest

## Notes

*If we believed in walking down life's beaten path...*
*we would seldom make any tracks of our own.*
~Victor McGuire

*There will come a time when you believe everything is finished.*
*That will be the beginning.*
~Anonymous

## About | The Author

Mariam MacGregor has a BA in Management from Gettysburg College and a MS in Student Affairs in Higher Education from Colorado State University. She is a licensed school counselor in the state of Colorado. She chose to focus on leadership education with at-risk adolescents after six years of working with student leadership development at the college level.

Prior to working in secondary education, she served as Associate Director of Student Activities/Leadership Development Director at Metropolitan State College of Denver; Assistant Director, Center for Student Leadership at Santa Clara University; and Assistant Director for Leadership and Student Organizations at Syracuse University.